Martin Lewis, Money Saving Expert, is a 34-year-old ultra-specialised journalist and TV presenter who grew up in Cheshire and now lives in West London. He spends his life focusing on how to cut bills without cutting back.

Martin is in constant demand on television and radio. He has his own series, *Make Me Rich*, on ITV1 as well as being the Money Saving Expert on *Tonight with Trevor McDonald*, BBC1's *The One Show* and others. He is a national newspaper columnist and has monthly phone-ins on BBC Radio 2 and Talk Sport.

In 2003 he set up a completely free website: www.moneysavingexpert.com. Three years after its launch, without any advertising budget, a million people a month were using the site, making it the country's biggest independent money site.

Before focusing on MoneySaving, Martin worked in the BBC's Business Unit and has reported for BBC1, BBC Network Radio and even spent time as a Business Editor of Radio 4's *Today* programme. Prior to that he worked 'for the other side' as a City spin doctor, advising major companies on how to communicate, and dabbled in stand-up comedy to 'relieve the tedium'.

Martin has a postgraduate degree in Broadcast Journalism from Cardiff University and is a graduate of the London School of Economics.

'The Dumbledore of Debt' Paul Ross, *This Morning*
'The UK's biggest Financial Anorak' Paul Lewis, BBC Radio 4's *Moneybox*
'If anyone can help, it's this man. Martin Lewis knows more about credit cards than possibly anyone else in the country' Justin Rowlatt, BBC1 *Panorama*

Dedicated to the war generation, who learned to save money without a choice, and who pass on their knowledge so the rest of us may thrive.

THRIFTY WAYS
FOR MODERN DAYS

Handy hints on living better for less from
the community of MoneySavingExpert.com

EDITED BY MARTIN LEWIS, MONEY SAVING EXPERT

Vermilion
LONDON

3 5 7 9 10 8 6 4 2

Copyright © Martin Lewis 2006

Martin Lewis has asserted his moral right to be identified as the author
of this work in accordance with the Copyright, Design and Patents Act 1988.

First published in the United Kingdom in 2006 by Vermilion,
an imprint of Ebury Publishing
Random House UK Ltd.
Random House
20 Vauxhall Bridge Road
London SW1V 2SA

Random House Australia (Pty) Limited
20 Alfred Street, Milsons Point, Sydney,
New South Wales 2061, Australia

Random House New Zealand Limited
18 Poland Road, Glenfield,
Auckland 10, New Zealand

Random House (Pty) Limited
Isle of Houghton, Corner Boundary Road & Carse O'Gowrie, Houghton 2198, South Africa

Random House Publishers India Private Limited
301 World Trade Tower, Hotel Intercontinental Grand Complex, Barakhamba Lane, New Delhi 110 001, India

Random House UK Limited Reg. No. 954009
www.randomhouse.co.uk
Papers used by Vermilion are natural, recyclable products made from wood grown in sustainable forests.

A CIP catalogue record is available for this book from the British Library.

ISBN: 0091912776
ISBN 13: 9780091912772 (from January 2007)

Printed and bound in Great Britain by
Mackays of Chatham plc, Chatham, Kent

CONTENTS

This book is based on the collective knowledge of scores of people, who've added their suggestions, ideas and experience to the 'MoneySaving Old-Style' section of the Chat Forum of Consumer Revenge website MoneySavingExpert.com

The Old-Style board started when many older MoneySavers wanted to share their accumulated wisdom with a new generation. Since then it's developed into a discussion on living life cheaply, healthily, ethically and thriftily, with all generations together searching for a path to Old-Style bliss.

As the book is based on collective wisdom, Martin Lewis is donating all his proceeds from it to the MoneySavingExpert.com Charitable Fund.

ACKNOWLEDGEMENTS

I don't truly consider this book to be mine, so it's rather strange to be writing the acknowledgements. This is a community's book, written from the contributions of a huge range of people to the discussions on the 'Old-Style' board, part of the Chat Forums of my website MoneySavingExpert.com

I must admit a great pride that such a community has formed, developed its own cohesive philosophy and now thrives; helping each other and newbies. So without doubt the first thanks must go to all the regulars, irregulars, occasionals and one-off posters. It is literally impossible to thank everyone, so I've picked at random a representative of the most common posters, and I apologise to those who've been omitted.

Old-Style thanks: Penny-Pincher, halloweenqueen, apprentice tycoon, lynzpower Thriftlady, Murtle, moggins, oops a daisy, purpleprincess, Crispy Ambulance, black-saturn, Snowy Owl, Queenie, Rikki, wigginsmum, VickyA, purplemoon, Bogof_Babe, Ticklemouse and RacyRed.

I'd also like to thank all the volunteer Board Guides who've kept the information easy to find, and compiled wonderful reference lists, many of which are detailed in this book: Squeaky, Arkonite Babe, Pink-winged, Gingham Ribbon, Cathy, Judi, Galtizz and Fran.

For the book itself, huge thanks go to Sue Hayward. Sue is a consumer journalist who researched, read and compiled the bulk of the information from the forums, and organised it into book form for me to edit. Without her work, this book wouldn't exist.

Martin Lewis, Money Saving Expert

FOREWORD: WHY I'M NOT AN OLD-STYLER

So, my picture's on the front cover, it's about MoneySaving, comes from my website and I'm the editor of this book, but the first thing I'm doing is shouting, 'I'm not an Old-Styler'. Confused? Well, of course MoneySaving is my thing, but within this context I suppose I should say MoneySaving New-Style is my thing.

New-Style is all about cutting your bills without cutting back, living your life exactly the same way yet paying less for it. It's about leaving you with more money to spend on yourself or pay off your debts, and indeed that's what my book *The Money Diet* and most of MoneySavingExpert.com is about.

Old-Style is different. The Old-Style board started when many older MoneySavers wanted to share their accumulated wisdom with a new generation. It's since developed into a discussion on living life cheaply, healthily, ethically and thriftily, with all generations searching together for a path to Old-Style wisdom.

These thrifty ways implicitly involve a change in lifestyle. New-Style is about putting every penny into *your* pocket rather than that of companies, yet with Old-Style you also deliberately choose to live life a different way. There are two main reasons for adopting this technique:

Necessity. Old-Style is fantastic for those with debt or other money problems who need to make extra savings to get back on track. It boosts your budget, but does require work and attention. Yet those who need to work hard on their finances tend to be more time-rich than money-rich, so it's the perfect solution, even with the necessary sacrifices.

Lifestyle choice. Many Old-Stylers don't do it just to save money; they do it because they believe in the de-cluttered, less consumerist, greener lifestyle it provides.

As you'd expect from a Money Saving Expert, I don't have problem debts. Thus, for me, it's a question of whether I choose to live an Old-Style life. Sometimes I don't – occasionally I even look askance at suggestions – yet equally there are some wonderful ideas that I've adopted.

I've learned much from Old-Stylers, and I wanted to store and share that wisdom. For those whose finances are sorted, a pick-and-mix approach to Old-Style is perfect. Take what you like, leave what you don't. There are many hugely powerful tips in Old-Style – but some aren't for me.

Martin Lewis, Money Saving Expert

WHAT IS OLD-STYLE MONEYSAVING?

It's all about depending on older, more basic and cheaper ways of running the home, not relying so much on modern consumerism, processed foods or off-the-shelf solutions. It's a do-it-yourself way of living.

Where Did it Come from?

The Old-Style board was started in the www.moneysavingexpert.com forums on 22 May 2004. It stemmed from a discussion about 'Could we live like during World War II?' and then morphed into a mix of MoneySaving and anti-consumerism. Many joined in and requested that I give it a section of its own.

Since then it's seen over 5,000 different discussions containing over 100,000 posts (written contributions) on everything from cleaning, cooking, buying clothes, DIY, gifts and presents, beauty treatments, recycling – you name it; there's pretty much an Old-Style way to do everything.

But Old-Style isn't all old; after all, it stems from the Internet. It utilises modern things like slow cookers, microwaves, bread-makers and more. It loves to reuse, reduce, recycle. It saves money (and, by coincidence, time and energy) by cooking double and freezing. What's old is that it tries not to rely on ready-made, instant lifestyles. It tries to shop with thrift in mind without blindly throwing the nearest and easiest thing into the shopping basket. And it always glances at the total on the till to set and keep budgets. Finally, it makes us ask ourselves questions like 'Is this something I would *like* to have, or is it something *genuinely useful*?'

How Old-Stylers Sum up 'Old-Style'

Old-Style for the sake of Old-Style is daft. But buying all the latest and greatest 'cleanse-while-you-sleep-spray-on-no-wipe-just-£1.99-stinks-your-house-out-and-takes-your-skin-off' is even dafter, especially since with half of those wonder cleaners you pay for all the advertising and fancy packaging the manufacturers have to do to catch customers. Finding the balance between what used to work in the olden days and what technological advances have been added since, without compromising the environment we all have to live in, is what I would call good Old-Style.

It's about thriftiness. My concept of 'Old-Style' is that it refers to 'old-fashioned' thriftiness, not necessarily using old cleaning techniques. It's about not spending money thoughtlessly on convenience foods or cleaning products (though you may want to sometimes when appropriate!)

Old-Style isn't necessarily about doing without. It's about living within one's means. All of my friends think I have rather a lot of money because I have so many lovely things at home – I just 'forget' to tell them that all of the dressings on my bed (throw from the White Company in a clearance sale, duvet cover and pillowcases 80 per cent off from Laura Ashley, pillows from eBay etc.) cost less than the amount of money that they've just spent on one throw!

OLD-STYLE CHALLENGES

Motivation is a great aid to Old-Style, thus a series of challenges has grown up. The spirit isn't to outdo each other, but it encourages a bit of experimentation. The pride isn't in beating the rest, but having discovered something new that others can share in.

Here are just a couple of the challenges.

Store Cupboard Challenge

Most of us are guilty of going to the supermarket even when we have a freezer or cupboard full of ingredients which could be used to make a meal. So this challenge stems from the desire to use up stuff before buying any more. When you're left with a tin of kidney beans, two eggs and a bit of cheese, it's tough to make a meal, but where there's an Old-Styler there's a way!

To do the challenge, come up with a recipe once a week that utilises ingredients you find in your kitchen cupboard or freezer. The older and nearer the use-by date of goods, the better. (This is also done on the Old-Style boards so you can read past ideas – go to www.moneysavingexpert.com/osstorecupboard)

Pin Money Savings

This is a true throwback to a bygone age. The old adage 'Take care of the pennies and the pounds will take care of themselves' is as true today as it's ever been, and so is the Old-Style idea of 'pin money', tucking away pennies to buy the odd luxury. Way back when, the pin money literally saved the day when families lived payday to payday or the breadwinner was made redundant.

First, you need a goal. You need to think about what you want to save for. Maybe it's something relatively small that would actually help you to save more money in the future, such as the Old-Styler cook's Holy Grail bread-maker.

Maybe you wish for something larger – a family holiday? A dishwasher? A newer car? These items may take longer to save up for, but they are still attainable.

Where is Your Pin Money Coming From?

A variety of ways:

◆ *Coupons/Vouchers. They're in newspapers, online, in leaflet stacks and more – grab them. Many supermarkets accept a whole range, including other supermarkets' vouchers, and sometimes they'll let you use coupons for goods you're not even purchasing. You can't bank on coupons when you draw up your household budget, so view them as a bonus. If you normally spend £50 per week on groceries and that week you have coupons which reduce your bill by £6, that £6 becomes your pin money savings. Put the same value of the coupons into your pin money.*

◆ *BOGOFs. If it's on your usual shopping list and you are able to get it on a buy one get one free, put the cash value of the saving into your pin money.*

◆ *Freebies. You can't bank on freebies to provide your gift needs (gift purchases are already accounted for in your budget planning) so they are also a bonus – the cash equivalent can go into your pin money. For much more on this see www.moneysavingexpert.com/freebiesboard*

◆ *The monthly food challenge. Take a look through the Store Cupboard Challenge and/or the Grocery Challenge. If you find your food bill reducing, put that extra into your pin money.*

◆ *Cleaning. If you use vinegar as a fabric softener, for example, work out the saving (you'll need to deduct the cost of the vinegar you are replacing it with) and put that amount into your pin money. (See Chapter 1, 'Cleaning'.)*

◆ *Make it from scratch. Look through the recipe collection (Chapter 8) and see if you can make it/bake it cheaper.*

At the end of each month, empty out your pin money and transfer it to a savings account so it can begin to earn a bit of interest (more pin money!) At the start of the next month, you will know how much you've shaved off your basic grocery bill (this applies to the food/fabric softener example, not those *unbankable* freebies/bogofs/coupons), so begin by putting *that* into your pin money.

What if things are soooo tight that every saving you make each week can't be put away because it's needed elsewhere?
Not a problem. You can still keep a record but instead of cash this will be your 'virtual' savings. It will be very encouraging to see how much you are 'saving' by making small changes, even if you can't put away the actual cash.

If you have already absorbed these savings into your budget and recalculated accordingly, that's okay. This challenge still applies because any new ideas/tips that you pick up can now be utilised for your pin money.

ALWAYS MAKE SURE OLD-STYLE IS YOUR-STYLE . . .

Just a quick word of warning before you start the Old-Style voyage. Do remember that the suggestions and solutions in this book come from a huge body of people, and what works for one won't necessarily work for all. If you're trying a solution on something valuable, sensitive or precious (and that includes yourself and kids), then always do a little safety test first before going the whole hog. Be careful and check that all actions are safe and right for your situation.

Remember, in the end the responsibility falls to you, so ruining your delicate flooring by using too much of the wrong thing certainly isn't Old-Style . . .

CUTTING YOUR BILLS WITHOUT CUTTING BACK: MARTIN'S FIVE TOP TASTER TIPS

Old-Style is about thrifty tricks to make little savings that, when combined, add up to a whopping great big life-style changing lump. Yet it's equally important to concentrate on the big stuff too and that's what New-Style MoneySaving is all out about – cutting the cost of things without changing your lifestyle, simply by being a better consumer. The average person in the UK could give themselves an equivalent of a 25 per cent pay rise by doing this effectively. While it's not the focus of this book, it's important to use Old-Style and New-Style in conjuction with each other. Thus, as a taster, here are five of the top places to start.

1. Mortgage Makeover – Ensure You've Got the Lowest Rate Possible

Remortgaging is the biggest single MoneySaving activity possible – the financial equivalent of liposuction – rapidly saving you £1000s. For each 1 per cent you cut off the rate on a £100,000 mortgage, you'll save around £80 a month. To make the saving is easy: simply find a mortgage broker which is 'fees-free' and 'whole of market' to guide you through the process and you'll get top advice without paying a penny.

Typical Saving: £1,200 per year

More info: www.moneysavingexpert.com/mortgagebrokers

2. Home and Car Insurance Cost Cutting

Rather than spending hours trying to find the cheapest insurance provider, use screen-scraping websites like Confused or Insuresupermarket. Here you enter your details and they whiz them to scores of brokers and direct sellers to find you the very cheapest quote. This effectively automates the shopping around for you, so you've scanned hundreds of companies in minutes.

Typical Saving: combined £600 per year

More info: www.moneysavingexpert.com/carinsurance
www.moneysavingexpert.com/homeinsurance

3. Use a Cheaper Energy Supplier and Get Paid for Switching to it

It's possible to cut your energy bills by up to 25 per cent simply by changing to a cheaper supplier. To do this, use a free phone or Internet comparison service such as Energyhelpline or UK Power. Here you simply tell them your postcode and your current bills and they calculate the very cheapest provider for you. Or you can opt for the cheapest green supplier of energy instead. Also, if you ask for it or use the correct web link, they will pay you a cut of their 'switching' commission in the form of cashback on top.

Typical Saving: £150 per year

More info: www.moneysavingexpert.com/energy

4. Pay More than 5 per cent Interest on Your Credit Card? Get Late Payment Fines? Stop!

Let's stop the fines first: set up a Direct Debit, even if just for the minimum repayment (you can always pay more on top). For those whose debts cost over 5 per cent, do a balance transfer if you can. This is where you get a new credit card that pays off the debts on the old cards for you, hopefully at a cheaper rate. The savings are massive. Even if you can't get new credit, it's still possible to make big savings simply by asking your current credit providers if they will allow you to shift debt to them at a cheaper rate via a technique I call the credit card shuffle.

Typical Saving: £500 per year

More info: www.moneysavingexpert.com/balancetransfers
www.moneysavingexpert.com/shuffle

5. Batter Down the Cost of Your Annual Mobile Phone Contract

There's a secret set of prices mobile phone companies don't tell us about, yet you can access them with a little chutzpah. All it takes is threatening to leave at the end of your contract period, and offers magically appear which are much better than those typically mentioned.

Typical Saving: £300 per year

More info: www.moneysavingexpert.com/batterdown

These are just the tip of the iceberg. All these savings are just for starters. Almost everywhere you spend money, it's possible to cut down your bills without any lifestyle change. Whether it's childcare vouchers, home phones, contact lenses, Internet shopping, ISAs, flights, broadband, banking, savings or holidays, there are methods to save money.

It's well worth doing these in conjunction with this book's thrifty tips. For more details on all these New-Style ways to save, either read *The Money Diet* or visit www.moneysavingexpert.com

DO YOU SPEND MORE THAN YOU EARN... OR EARN MORE THAN YOU SPEND...?

Before we begin with thrifty tricks, it's crucially important to understand your own money situation. The first step is to realistically assess how much money you've got coming in and going out. Once that's sorted, you can start making as many changes as you can, which you won't even notice. I've pilfered bits here from my book *The Money Diet* to get us going. Don't worry though; after this we're full speed ahead with Old-Style...

BUDGET - PREPARE YOUR POCKET (COURTESY OF *THE MONEY DIET*)

'I'm always skint after Christmas'

Sitting in a bar one cold January evening with a well-paid friend who works in the City, I suggested we order some food. She turned to me and

said, 'Would you mind if we just got drinks? I'm skint.' Now I was quite
surprised by this. Why was she skint? Her answer: 'Christmas, of course.'

'And?' I asked again.

'What do you mean, and?' she said. 'It's just been Christmas. I've
spent loads of money. I'm skint.'

Now, you're probably thinking, what's he going on about?
Christmas is a good reason for spending – the festivities, the presents,
going out, office parties, meeting people, and the excuse to spend and
shop. So I'd like to point out a little fact – Christmas happens on 25
December every year; it's not unexpected. Yet many people try to pay
for it out of December's money, and this is often doomed to failure –
leaving a post-Christmas credit hangover to accompany alcohol's
mists. This isn't just a Christmas phenomenon: it applies to tax bills,
summer holidays and a lot more.

Avoid a Spiralling Financial Descent

Let's look at the potential consequences of what my friend did.

All her spending on food, drink, gifts and décor was in the pre-
Christmas run-up – the time when shops traditionally charge the most.
When January rolls round, the sales are on and it's the cheapest time
to buy. In her job she has to look good and feels the need to buy
designer clothing. But she has no money left in January to take
advantage of the bargains, so she has to wait and buy her clothes later
in the year instead. This means it costs her a lot more, dropping her
finances down yet another step. So by the time next Christmas arrives,
she's still paying for the last one. And thus starts the spiral.

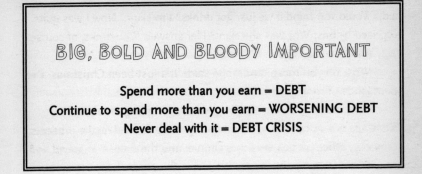

BIG, BOLD AND BLOODY IMPORTANT

Spend more than you earn = DEBT
Continue to spend more than you earn = WORSENING DEBT
Never deal with it = DEBT CRISIS

Budget, Plan, Prepare

The weapons to fight downward-spiralling finances are budget, plan and prepare. These aren't necessarily easy, but are easily necessary. Even those lucky enough to have a bigger income than expenditure will benefit.

A FOUR-STEP 'HAPPINESS' PLAN

There are four simple steps to keep your expenditure below your income. You can follow these alone or as part of a couple or family. Just be consistent – if you start them for a couple, make sure you fill in the total spending for both, down to the smallest article of clothing. Do it alone, then only put in your proportion of any rent or mortgage.

Step 1: Don't Trust Your Bank Account

Bank accounts are devious and cunning beasts. When you get paid, they seduce you into believing the cash in there is the cash you have available to spend. Yet this wanton temptation is a terrible vice. Bank accounts lie!

We spend money in many ways and over many time periods. Purchases are daily, weekly, monthly or one-offs. However, your bank account presents only a snapshot of how much money is in your account at that moment. It ignores where you are in your money cycle – receiving your salary and paying your bills don't necessarily coincide. It also forgets that although Christmas comes but once a year, its cost should be spread all year round; as should that of holidays. Yet knowing the logic is no protection, so let's move on to step 2.

Step 2: Discover What Your Real Monthly Spend is

This isn't as obvious as it seems, as it's important to incorporate all the real demands on your income. To help, I've developed the Money Diet Monthly Calorie Counter.

All you have to do is fill it in. After each category you can choose whether to enter the spending as per week, per month or per year – just fill in whichever is appropriate. Don't panic if you don't know exactly how much you spend on something. A good guess is better than giving up.

For a free, fully automated version of this, go to
www.moneysavingexpert.com/budgeting

Some pointers:

◆ *Only count things once. Some spending may overlap — if you've already counted it, don't count it again.*

◆ *Overestimation is better than underestimation. Honesty pays dividends. Fight that very human temptation to lie to yourself about your spending, and if you're not sure, pick more, not less. If you overestimate you'll have money left over rather than still being short.*

◆ *Don't forget anything. There's bound to be something you spend on that's not on the list — have a think and make sure you fit it in, either in an 'others' section or the 'odds and sods' at the end. If you're struggling, do it over a week, as each day's activities should act as a reminder of where your cash goes.*

◆ *MoneySave while you write. As well as counting the calories as you write the numbers down, always ask yourself, 'Is this really the best deal I can get?'*

Okay — now fill in just Part A of the chart. Once this is completed, work out what your real monthly spending is by filling in Part B, the 'monthly total' column. To do this you will (probably) need a calculator.

◆ *For things in the Per Week column: Multiply the amount by 4.33 (the average number of weeks in a month) and put the answer in the 'monthly total' column.*

◆ *For things in the Per Month column: Move the answer straight over to the 'monthly total' column.*

◆ *For things in the Per Year column: Divide the amount by 12 and put the answer in the 'monthly total' column.*

Now total up each section and write the answer below.

Home total per month   _____

Insurance total per month   _____

Eats, Drinks & Smokes total per month   _____

Transport and Travel total per month   _____

Debt Repayments total per month   _____

Savings & Investments total per month   _____

Family total per month   _____

Fun and Frolics total per month   _____

Big One-offs total per month   _____

Clothes total per month   _____

Education, Courses and Classes total per month   _____

Odds and Sods total per month   _____

Total Monthly Expenditure   _____

Money Diet Monthly Calorie Counter					
	FILL IN FOR PART A			PART B	PART C
	Per week	Per month	Per year	Monthly total	Monthly desired
HOME					
Mortgage/Rent					
Household maintenance					
Home & contents insurance					
Council tax					
Water rates/Meter					
Gas bill					
Electricity bill					
Oil bill					
Home phone bill					
Internet bill					
Mobile phone bill(s)					
Cleaning products/cleaner					
Garden maintenance					
Other home					
TOTAL HOME					
INSURANCE					
Level-term assurance					
Private medical insurance					
Healthcare cashback scheme					
Pet insurance					
Travel insurance					
Gas & plumbing cover					
Other insurance					
TOTAL INSURANCE					

Money Diet Monthly Calorie Counter

	FILL IN FOR PART A			PART B	PART C
	Per week	Per month	Per year	Monthly total	Monthly desired
EATS, DRINKS & SMOKES					
Food shopping					
Eating out					
Coffee/sandwiches out					
Meals at work					
Pet food					
Drink for home					
Drinking out					
Smoking					
Other eats, drinks & smokes					
TOTAL EATS					
TRANSPORT AND TRAVEL					
Rail/bus/coach/taxi					
Car maintenance					
Car insurance					
Car tax					
Petrol					
Parking					
AA/RAC membership					
Other car					
TOTAL TRANSPORT					
DEBT REPAYMENTS (just the average amount repaid, not the total debt)					
Car loan repayments					
Personal loan repayment					
HP repayments					
Credit card repayment					
Other loan repayment					
TOTAL DEBT REPAYMENTS					

(REMEMBER DO NOT DOUBLE COUNT: If you've noted your spending elsewhere, then don't add it in the debt repayment column)

Money Diet Monthly Calorie Counter					
	FILL IN FOR PART A			**PART B**	**PART C**
	Per week	Per month	Per year	Monthly total	Monthly desired
SAVINGS & INVESTMENTS (how much you pay in, not how much is in there)					
Saving schemes					
Mini cash ISAs					
Investments					
Buying shares					
Pension payments					
Other savings/investments					
TOTAL SAVINGS					
FAMILY					
Childcare/playschemes					
Babysitting					
Children's travel					
Laundry/dry cleaning					
School meals					
Pocket money					
Nappies/baby extras (e.g. baby wipes)					
Other family					
TOTAL FAMILY					
FUN AND FROLICS					
Hobbies					
Pet costs					
Fitness/sports/gym					
Shopping for fun					
Big days out					
Books/music/DVDs/ computer games					
Cinema/theatre trips					
Family days out					
NTL/Sky subscription					
TV licence					
DVD/video rental					
Other fun and frolics					
TOTAL FUN AND FROLICS					

Money Diet Monthly Calorie Counter

	FILL IN FOR PART A			PART B	PART C
	Per week	Per month	Per year	Monthly total	Monthly desired
BIG ONE-OFFS (for things spent less than once a year, divide the total by the number of years and put it in the per year column)					
Cost of Christmas					
Cost of summer holiday					
Cost of winter holiday					
Cost of birthdays					
Cost of new sofa/kitchen/ TV/other electrical					
Other big one-offs					
TOTAL BIG ONE-OFFS					
CLOTHES					
New clothes					
New children's clothes					
Work clothes					
Other clothes					
TOTAL CLOTHES					
EDUCATION, COURSES AND CLASSES					
Your courses/classes					
School fees					
University tuition fees					
Other education costs					
TOTAL EDUCATION					
ODDS AND SODS (anything that doesn't fit anywhere else)					
Regular charity donations					
Tax and NI provisions (self-employed only)					
Newspapers & magazines					
Dentistry					
Optical bills					
Complementary therapies					
Haircuts					
Beauty treatments					
Other odds and sods					
TOTAL ODDS AND SODS					

Step 3: Work Out What You Can Spend Each Month

You've got your answer... are you shocked? Don't worry – almost everyone is. It's almost always more than you thought. That's because lots of money floats away through Direct Debits, standing orders and cheques without really entering our consciousness. Plus those big one-offs aren't usually counted this way, so when you add them in it can hurt.

Don't panic, though. Let's see if your spending is affordable by discovering what your income is. It shouldn't be as tough, but here's a table to help. All figures should be after tax.

How much do you earn each month?	
Income	After tax monthly earnings*
Average earnings from employment/ self-employment	
Incomes taken each month from savings/investments	
Pensions and annuity payouts (state and private)	
Benefits, including child benefit, child tax credit, income support, council tax benefit	
Gifts or help from family or friends	
Other	
TOTAL	

*If the income isn't monthly, then use the same system as in the Calorie Counter (previous pages) to work out the monthly equivalent you receive.
*If you're self-employed, then use untaxed earnings and fill in the tax and NI provisions in the Calorie Counter.

Happiness!

Your income is bigger than your expenditure – 'happiness'. HOORAH!
Apart from jumping up and down for joy, you're also relatively safe in the
knowledge you can afford to save a little more or treat yourself a little
better. However, that isn't a reason not to budget or plan. Just because
you have spare cash doesn't mean you should throw it away. In one
Make Me Rich makeover, I found a family who were 'happy'. Another
£12,000 a year, by being better consumers, made them happier!

Misery!

Your expenditure is bigger than your income – 'misery'. This tends to
be a more common outcome. You're probably saying 'Wooaaah!' – or
maybe something more colourful – 'do I really overspend by that
much?' And you're right to be shocked because it is a problem.
Continued overspending isn't sustainable: you will get into debt, with
more and more of your salary going to pay interest, leaving less and
less to spend, making it even worse. It's time to cut your expenditure.

There are three ways:

◆   *Pain-free. This is my prime aim. Use the cheapest and best-value
    products and services to mash down your spending. Before you do
    anything else, make the product changes and then redo the table
    with the new figures. Hopefully, it'll reduce your personal deficit.*

◆   *Pain-ful. If switching products isn't enough, then it's ouch time – you
    need to cut your spending. This has to be done honestly, though;
    don't arbitrarily cut down your paper spending unless you mean it. If
    you then think 'Damn it' and end up spending more than you've put
    aside, this whole exercise is lost.*

◆ *Painless pain. There are many spending cuts that shouldn't hurt much and most of them are here in Old-Style – saving a little less; eating out a little less; taking control of your phone habit; turning the lights off as soon as you leave the room; taking videos/DVDs back to the rental shop on time; filling the petrol tank when it's still half-full, to give you time to shop around for the cheapest. These are the types of thing people typically laugh at when they explain to me how bad they are with money. Stop laughing. Pay attention to them. Then start smiling.*

All spending reductions hurt. However, I make no apology for saying that they are necessary and you must spend within your means. This is about continually running through your expenditure until you have cut out everything you can.

Step 4: Trust Your Piggybank

Your budget is set. Now we need to make it as easy as possible to stick to it. To do that we must turn 'It's the beginning of the month, I can go shopping, hoorah!' into 'It's the end of the month, I've got money left, I'll go shopping.'

You may laugh at the thought of ever having money left at the end of the month, yet stop spending at the beginning of it and there may be more than you think. The trick is to take temptation out of your path with a wee bit of organisation.

This is where my piggybanking comes into action. It's about putting your money into different piggybanks. In practical terms, these are different bank accounts, each designated for certain types of spending. Every month, as soon as you are paid, siphon off the right proportion of money (according to your planned budget) into each of these accounts.

The accounts you choose depend on your particular spending patterns, but let me use an example to explain. Let's assume you set up the following five accounts in addition to your normal day-to-day account:

◆   *Bills (including mortgage)*
◆   *Family food*
◆   *Holidays*
◆   *Christmas*
◆   *Savings*

When I say different accounts, I literally mean using separate current accounts at your bank. Even better, put the cash in a savings account (preferably high-interest) with easy withdrawal facilities so it will earn decent interest too. There's usually no problem having more than one account at one bank, and there's definitely no problem having a few accounts at different banks. You could even do it just by allocating amounts on a computer or on paper, as long as you keep it up to date and stick to your plan. Do whatever you feel most comfortable with.

Once you have the new account, automate moving the budgeted amount of money there on the day (or day after, to be safe) you are paid. This can be done by Direct Debit, standing order or manually.

The goal here is to leave in your main account only the money available to spend, and no more. The other accounts will contain the money to meet specific demands on your cash. This may mean that now you can see you can't afford the first-class holiday you wanted, but in reality you couldn't before either. At least now you'll vacation with the peace of mind that you won't suffer the rest of the year because of it. Do this and your bank account will finally be trustworthy.

Chapter 1

 CLEANING

Forgive a wee bit of sentimentality. You may think 'cleaning' a strange place to start, yet it was cleaning that made me create 'Old-Style' in the first place. I read a discussion in the Chat Forum of such rich information and a radically different approach that I thought 'Wow! That deserves some space of its own.' Hence Old-Style was born... and so I'm starting with cleaning here too, so the book comes to life through the same route. Now enough from me, over to the Old-Stylers.

Martin

People waste a fortune on expensive branding and packaging when it comes to cleaning. Each household spends an average £1,000 a year on products that promise to degrease, unblock, dissolve and literally wash away dirt and grime better than anything we've ever used before. But in the real world it's just a way to make us pay more for ingredients we've been using for years. Of course they may smell fancy, but as you'll discover you can always add a bit of essential oil to your cleaning products to get the same effect.

THE OLD-STYLE TOP FIVE CLEANERS

1. White Vinegar

Not the brown Sarsons stuff you stick on your chips

Definitely the number-one Old-Style favourite cleaner. It's cheap, cheerful and multi-purpose, and a few drops of your favourite essential oil will mask any lingering smells. White vinegar, also known as 'distilled' vinegar, is colourless, and you can use it for everything from unblocking sinks and removing limescale to cleaning worktops – and even in place of fabric conditioner to fluff up your towels in the wash.

Where to Buy it

Your local supermarket: Asda sells 500ml bottles for under 50p, but for the best value find a Chinese or Asian supermarket where you can get a 5 litre container for under £2. Or go to one of those big cash-and-carry places like Makro (www.makro.co.uk) where you can pick up 5 litres of the stuff for between £3 and £4.

What Does it Do?

◆   *Unblocks sinks (when mixed with bicarbonate of soda)*
◆   *Household cleaner – mix with water and stick in an old spray container to use on worktops, bathrooms and kitchens*
◆   *De-scaler – use in kettles, your coffee maker jug, vases and down the loo*
◆   *Flushes out washing machines and dishwashers and helps prevent limescale build-up*

How Much to Use?

Half water, half vinegar in a spray container is the best mix for cleaning surfaces. Use it neat when poured down sinks to clear clogs or when using to flush out washing machines and dishwashers.

2. Bicarbonate of Soda (Bicarb)

Yep, it's the same stuff you stick in your cakes and cookies to make them rise!

Where to Buy it

Dead easy to get hold of, most supermarkets stock it in the home baking aisle. A small 200g pot costs way less than a pound in Tesco, Asda or Sainsbury's. But, for bulk buys, find your local Chinese or Asian supermarket – depending on where you live, you can pick up 5kg packs for under £3.

What Does it Do?

- Works on household stains – great for de-scaling teacups and teapots
- Great cleaner for fridges and microwaves
- Deodoriser – gets rid of stinks and smells in the fridge

How Much to Use?

You don't need much – less than a teaspoon for each cup or mug if you're using it to 'de-scale', then add a splash of water and leave to soak. For cleaning the gunk off the inside of oven doors, make a paste from a couple of teaspoons of bicarb and a small amount of water until it's a fairly thick consistency. Use it neat to rid the fridge of smells – stick a couple of tablespoons in a small pot at the back of the fridge.

3. Washing Powder

Keep a box of dirt cheap 'value' washing powder in the cupboard for everyday household use

Where to Buy it
Tesco sells a 1kg box of value washing powder for under £1 but you can buy cheap own brand 'no frills' style washing powder in most super-markets.

What Does it Do?
◆ *Stain remover – gets rid of tea stains in cups and mugs*
◆ *De-greaser – cleans up your gunked-up pots and pans and oven trays*
◆ *Boil it up in burnt pans to bring them up sparkling clean*

How Much to Use?
Similar to the amounts for bicarb – less than a teaspoon in mugs and cups with a dash of water to get rid of stains. A few tablespoons in a greasy oven tray with hot water should be enough to get it sparkling clean.

4. Cola

Multi-purpose stuff: drink it and when it's flat use it round the house!

Where to Buy it
Either use up the flat stuff or buy economy or value cola, literally
pennies for a 2 litre bottle in Tesco. Less than a tenth of the price of a
toilet cleaner and does the job even better!

What Does it Do?
◆   *Chuck it down the loo for a sparkling clean*
◆   *Shifts burnt-on food on saucepans*

5. Borax

From household cleaning to laundry – an all-round household cleaner

Where to Buy it
You can get a 750g box for under £2 in some branches of Boots in the
household aisle; some branches of Wilkinsons stock it or buy from the
Dri-Pak website (www.dri-pak.co.uk).

What Does it Do?
◆   *Stain remover for clothes*
◆   *Toilet cleaner*
◆   *Cleans cookers*

OLD-STYLE CLEANING VERSUS BRANDED PRODUCT CLEANING

Cost-wise, here's what you can save cleaning your house the Old-Style way – the rough cost of your monthly shopping basket of cleaning products. Swap the brand names for the Old-Style products every month and you'll save £100s a year.

Product	Brand Product	Old-Style Cleaner	Saving
Surface cleaner	Branded kitchen cleaner spray (£1.22 for 500ml)	White vinegar (£2 for 5 litres)	£2.04 per litre
Loo cleaner	Branded toilet cleaner (96p for 750ml)	Value cola (14p for 2 litres)	82p
Greasy dishes de-gunker	Branded power spray (£2.44 for 375ml)	Value washing powder (50p per 1kg biological automatic)	£1.94
Fridge deodoriser	Branded fridge gem deodoriser (£1.98)	Bicarbonate of soda (44p a tub)	£1.54
Cooker cleaner	Branded oven cleaner (£1.78 for 300ml)	Bicarbonate of soda (44p a tub)	£1.34
Furniture wipes	Branded furniture wipes (£2.98 for 40)	Value baby wipes (89p for 80)	£2.09
Window cleaner	Branded window cleaning spray (£1.14 for 500ml)	Vinegar and water in spray bottle (50p for 500ml)	64p

Sink unblocker	Branded sink and plughole unblocker (£2.99 for 500ml)	Vinegar and bicarb (50p for bottle of vinegar and 44p a tub of bicarb)	£2.05
	TOTAL COST	**TOTAL COST**	**TOTAL SAVING**
	£16.71	£4.25	£12.46

CLEAN YOUR HOUSE THE OLD-STYLE WAY

So what are you waiting for? You've got your vital ingredients – here's how to get your pad or palace sparkling like a new pin the Old-Style way!

Start from 'top' to 'bottom' in each room, quite literally, cleaning from the top so the dust and dirt falls down (rather than cleaning the floors first and having dust and muck land on them after you've wiped down the CD shelf).

Lounge and Dining Room

What You'll Need
- Baby wipes ('value' version from the supermarket)
- Home-made polish (lemon juice and olive oil)
- Old newspapers (the free ones that come through the door)
- White vinegar
- Old socks, dusters, tea towels, toothbrushes etc.
- A lemon

◆   *Used tumble dryer sheets*
◆   *Hot soapy water*

Light Bulbs

How filthy are these? Wondered why the room seemed dark and dingy all year round?

◆   *A quick 30-second tip is to get a damp (not wet!) cloth and put a couple of drops of your favourite essential oil on it. Always make sure the lights are switched off and the bulbs cold before doing this.*
◆   *Give a quick wipe over the light bulbs and radiators before switching them on. The heat will release the smell and they'll get a good clean. (Naturally this won't be as effective in summer and it's unlikely to work as well on energy-saving light bulbs as they don't get hot.)*

Woodwork

Get your dining table gleaming with some home-made polish. Forget the Mr Sheen and make your own by adding a drop of lemon juice to some olive oil – great for polishing up wood and your leather suite.

◆   *Just wipe it on, let it dry for a minute and buff it off.*
◆   *For stubborn marks like cup rings on wooden tables, use equal amounts of lemon juice and olive oil, rub gently into the stain and leave for a few hours before wiping off.*
◆   *If that won't shift it try dipping a damp cloth in some bicarbonate of soda and rubbing it gently into the mark. This stuff's a natural abrasive so don't go too mad! Wipe away the excess then polish as usual.*

Dusting

Cheap facial cleaning cloths are great to de-gunk CD cases, DVDs and book covers. Use them after you've already wiped your face with them for maximum value but, ladies, not after taking off your make-up! Cheap baby wipes do the same job and are great for cleaning light switches (just make sure they're not too wet!), computers, radiators and anything with those 'hard to reach' fiddly bits but not for use after cleaning your baby!

◆ *To dust the lounge try a damp micro-fibre cloth (you can pick these up cheaply at Lidl etc.). This saves money on polish and it actually picks up the dust instead of spreading it round the room. It works a treat for most surfaces in the home like mirrors, computer keyboards, furniture and walls.*

◆ *To get behind radiators use a long-handled micro-fibre fluffy duster (from the local pound shop) or hold a damp tea towel by the corner and dangle it behind the radiator, swing it around and the dust should stick to it or you can use a damp sock stuck on a wire coat hanger.*

◆ *Make sure you've got a stockpile of cleaning rags. Anything from cut-down jeans, old T-shirts and muslin rags to tatty tea towels can be used. Never bin those 'free' newspapers. They're great for scrunching up to clean windows and mirrors after spraying with a vinegar and water solution.*

◆ *Old toothbrushes come into their own for cleaning around the bottom of radiators (the bit where they disappear into the floor) and all those hard to get at nooks and crannies.*

Flooring

Laminate floors are so much easier to clean than carpets when it comes to mopping up spills.

◆ *For the best finish vacuum up the fluff, dog hairs and general mess and then get down on the floor armed with some good old-fashioned elbow grease and a bucket of hot water with a few drops of 'Zoflora' and wash the floor. Zoflora is a concentrated disinfectant and can be found in most supermarkets with the household cleaners or in the gardening section of DIY stores (it's a good disinfectant for drains).*

◆ *For scuff marks use a pencil eraser, and for those hard to budge, 'nothing will shift it' marks, go over them with a matching felt pen.*

Carpets

There's no miracle way to tackle carpets so grab yourself a bowl of warm water and a pair of marigolds and get down on your hands and knees.

◆ *With your gloves on, put your hands in the water, then shake off the excess and rub your hands in one direction on the carpet. Pulling towards you with your fingertips pressed firmly into the carpet is best. The hair will lift out and roll into sausage shapes for easy removal. Or you can do this using an old washing-up pad or cloth.*

◆ *Clean carpet stains by soaking with a solution of warm water and biological washing powder. Cover with a white towel and then walk on it until most of the water is absorbed and leave to dry.*

◆ *For smells, sprinkle the carpet with lots of bicarbonate of soda and*

vacuum up after 15 minutes – much cheaper than 'Shake 'n' Vac'.
For carpet dents where furniture's been standing, put an ice cube in
the hole till it melts then brush out.

For more about getting stains out of carpets, see 'Common Stains and
How to Get Rid of Them', page 51.

Windows

Start by rubbing a slice of lemon over the glass to get rid of greasy
marks, then spray with neat white vinegar and rub. The trick is to rub
the inside window up and down and the outside one from side to side
– this way any streaks are more easily spotted! While it's great to
encourage little ones to get into the habit of helping with the house-
work it's worth keeping an eye on them. One of the Old-Style
community noticed her young son trying to copy her window cleaning
using the inside of a banana after spotting her using a yellow duster!

Sofas

How to clean your sofa is a hot potato for Old-Stylers. While some
swear by baby wipes, others claim they can take the colour out of dark
sofas so it's always recommended that you do a patch test first. For a
cheap and cheerful version, check out a budget or value range like
Tesco or wait for the BOGOF (buy one, get one free) offers.

Saddle soap – which looks like an ordinary bar of soap but
contains added glycerine and moisturisers – is another option. Used
for years to clean horse leather saddles, it can be used to clean leather
sofas. It is sold in a tub as well as a solid block and is usually found in

outdoor adventure shops rather than supermarkets. Use a sponge to rub it into the grain, rinse the sponge out and wipe off the saddle soap. It's reckoned to remove even ground-in dirt and biro!

Television

Switch off the television before you clean it and make sure you don't get any liquid inside it. Get rid of the static by cleaning it with one part fabric conditioner and four parts water. Tumble dryer sheets can be reused for wiping over the television or computer screen to reduce static. For sticky marks everywhere try a quick squirt of WD40 and wipe off. Depending on the surface, either white spirit or hairspray can do the trick if you're out of WD40.

Computer

We eat over it, spill drinks over it and it's got more bacteria and bugs than your toilet – yes, it's your computer keyboard! Here's how to clean it properly. As with your television, always make sure it's switched off before you clean it and be careful not to get any liquid inside either the keyboard or the computer.

♦ *Take all the keys off. They should snap off pretty easily and can be cleaned individually in a bowl of soapy water, though be warned, you could give up the will to live before you're halfway through!*

♦ *Failing that, a damp toothbrush (keyboard disconnected of course) dipped in some soapy water can be rubbed over the keys, then these can be dried off with a cloth. Or you could use a make-up brush between the keys or even a little tub of warm soapy water with a handful of cotton buds.*

- Run the cotton bud in one direction along the rows of keys. At the end of each row, use tweezers or a skewer to flick out the remaining dust and debris that has gathered.
- Keep going until you've got rid of most of the gunk.
- Leave your keyboard to dry thoroughly before using it again.

The Kitchen

What You'll Need
- White vinegar
- Glycerine
- Soda crystals
- Washing powder
- Bicarbonate of soda

Great Kitchen Cleaners
- White vinegar and water mixed and stuck in an old spray bottle can be used as an all-round, all-purpose kitchen cleaner. Use it on worktops, windows, taps and even the floor. There's no definitive version for the recipe but most people go for one part vinegar to two parts water and add in a few drops of any essential oil. If you haven't got any oil add a dash of lemon juice.
- Use old washing-up pads and gloves to clean the kitchen and bathroom.
- Buy stainless steel pads and add a drop of washing-up liquid – they last forever and don't rust.

◆　*Or make your own scrubbing pads by saving all the nets that come with packs of oranges, lemons and mandarins, and when you have three or four you can scrunch them together and stitch them – voilà!*

Flush out the Dishwasher

◆　*Once a month half-fill a cup with white vinegar, pour it in one of the dishwasher trays and run a cycle on empty to flush out the limescale build-up. Or if you've run out of vinegar, two lemon halves on an empty wash will make it smell good too. Do it on the first day of every month and you'll never forget!*

◆　*And when you're washing your crocks, just because it says to use a whole tablet per wash on the packet doesn't mean you have to! Use half a tablet instead and you won't notice the difference.*

Defrost the Freezer

◆　*Wipe glycerine (which you can get from your local chemist) over the inside of the freezer after defrosting. This should help with the next defrost. Keeping it frost-free makes it more efficient to run.*

◆　*Keep the door shut. Sounds obvious but how many of us wander off leaving the door open? It wastes energy and takes time to get back to the optimum temperature. Don't put warm food into it as it makes it work twice as hard.*

De-scale the Washing Machine

◆　*Run an empty cycle on a boil wash with a cupful of white vinegar in the fabric conditioner drawer – it gets rid of limescale. Or do the same thing with a handful of soda crystals for a good old flush through.*

◆ Use a slug of vinegar in your final rinse instead of fabric conditioner – it makes your towels come up super soft. The vinegar seems to eradicate the soap residue, making everything light and fluffy. For anyone worried about smelling like they've spent all night in the local chippy, strangely enough you won't.

◆ Using vinegar won't hurt your machine and it's cheaper than fabric conditioner, but remember to use 'distilled white' vinegar, not the brown malt stuff which would stain.

Sinks and Drains

◆ Try a mild solution of white vinegar (with a bit of lemon juice or a drop of essential oil to mask the smell of vinegar) poured down the sink and rub the sink round with half a lemon.

◆ For clogs and slow-draining sinks, sprinkle some bicarb down the sink, then get a mug of vinegar and pour it down. It will fizz up out of the plug hole. Leave for half an hour or longer before flushing through with water.

◆ For outside drains a bottle of caustic soda poured down the drain will move a mountain and clean the drain out at the same time, but do wear a mask and gloves when handling it.

Taps and Draining Boards

◆ Mix about half a mug of white vinegar with baking powder and, as it's fizzing, pour over the draining board. Let it soak for a while and rinse off with water.

◆ To get taps looking new and sparkling, pour vinegar and lemon juice in a small plastic bag (about an egg cupful of the mix), and put the bag over the tap so the bottom of the tap is sitting in the mix. Stick an elastic band round it to keep the bag in place, then an hour later take it off and rinse and you're limescale free.

Grease and Gunk: Pots, Pans and the Oven

'Good old-fashioned soaking is underrated,' says the Old-Style community, so instead of scrubbing dishes encrusted with the cremated remains of yesterday's Sunday roast, just fill up with hot water and some cheap washing-up liquid and leave to soak.

◆ For oven tops, soak an old tea towel in warm water, lay it over the top of a crusty cooker and leave for half an hour. It helps shift the muck which can then be wiped off.

◆ For greasy oven dishes, dissolve a couple of cups of washing powder (bio is recommended but non-bio works too and, yes, it can be the 'value' stuff) in enough hot water to cover the dishes and oven shelves. Leave to soak overnight then rinse off to save spending hours scrubbing. Stick the grill pan in the dishwasher. If it doesn't shift the muck completely, make the washing powder paste thicker and paint it on with a paint brush.

◆ For the grill element in the oven, make a paste of water and biological washing powder or vinegar and bicarbonate of soda and paint it on. Leave on for a couple of hours, or overnight, and then rinse off with cold water.

◆ To clean the oven, wait till it's cooled down but still warm and run a vinegar-soaked cloth round the whole oven.

◆ For grime-encrusted ovens, try placing a large oven-proof bowl of boiling water with a lemon squeezed into it in a hot oven and let it boil away until it has almost boiled dry, say a couple of hours. Then right away, as soon as it's cool enough to touch, wipe it down with a solution of bicarbonate of soda and vinegar mixed in the water.

◆ For those brown marks on the door glass, use some bicarbonate of soda and lemon juice paste and a little elbow grease.

◆ For gas cooker hobs where the metal rings around the gas plate have gone black with carbonised gunk, shove them in the bath in the bio washing powder mix to come up like new.

◆ Baking trays and roasting tins – add a cup of biological washing powder to warm water and soak. You can remove tougher stains by heating gently on the hob for 10 minutes.

◆ Boil tartar sauce in water to remove the 'rainbow' effect from aluminium pans.

◆ To remove rust from cast-iron pans and woks, rub with the cut side of half a potato dipped in concentrated washing-up liquid. Rinse, then wipe with cooking oil and paper towel.

◆ To remove the tarnish from copper cookware, sprinkle with salt, cover with lemon juice or vinegar, then rub the affected area again. Rinse thoroughly and buff dry.

Don't Forget Your Appliances

The average small household appliance lasts just four years; make yours survive even longer by cleaning it.

Irons

◆ Get an iron cleaning stick. These are about the size of a lipstick. You warm the iron up (not hot though) and rub on the waxy stick which melts off any debris on the iron. It costs around £2 from places like John Lewis and makes the iron as good as new.

◆ A more Old-Style tip is to use a bar of soap and, while the iron is hot (but turned off), rub it all over the iron plate. It will stink, but let it cool a bit – not completely – and then rub it with a cloth. Don't attempt to rub off the muck with a scourer as it risks scratching the iron plate which might then snag on clothing. An added bonus of a clean plate is that your ironing is made easier – the iron will glide over the garments instead of sticking.

◆ A slick of petroleum jelly, a.k.a. Vaseline, round the steam holes will stop rust, but give it a good wipe before ironing.

To de-scale the iron and stop it dripping horrid splodgy brown water, especially when ironing white shirts, de-scale as you would with a kettle. Add a solution of water and white vinegar to the usual steam water chamber while the iron is hot but turned off. Leave that to 'stand' for roughly an hour then pour the solution out into a jug. If the holes are blocked on your iron plate then repeat the above, but this time place the iron, plate side down, on a wire rack (such as the grill pan rack) and let the hot, steamy solution work its way out of the holes.

Kettles

Clean the outside with vinegar and newspaper as you do with your windows or try baby oil for mirrored stainless steel versions. For the

inside, mix bicarb of soda with vinegar for a nice fizz and de-scale –
leave it overnight if you can.

Alternatively, use the cheapest vinegar you can find, pour in
enough to cover the element and come up to the 'minimum' line then
bring to the boil. Once the boiled vinegar has cooled a little, give the
inside of the kettle a quick scrub to get off any really tough limescale. It
then needs a good rinse and boil it a couple of times before using,
throwing away the water.

Microwave Magic

◆ *Put a bowl of vinegar on 'high', let it steam for a few minutes then*
   wipe out the microwave with a cloth dipped in the vinegar. Comes up
   spotless and non-smelly!
◆ *Another option is hot water with a tablespoon of bicarbonate of soda*
   in it. Stick it on high for five minutes and then wipe clean.
◆ *Get a fresh lemon, cut it in half and squeeze out the juice into a glass*
   bowl of warm water. Put the remains of the lemon into the bowl as
   well, run the microwave on defrost for 15 minutes, then wipe out with
   clean water.

Bathroom

What You'll Need

◆ *White vinegar*
◆ *Newspaper (the free ones that come through the door!)*
◆ *Bicarbonate of soda*

- Flat or cheap cola
- Lemon juice
- Cheap washing powder
- Car polishing wax
- Denture tablets (value ones from Tesco)
- Toothpaste (cheapest whitening one you can find)

Windows and Mirrors

For added sparkle mix one part vinegar to 10 parts water and spray on as you would your usual glass cleaner. This version won't evaporate as quickly as there's no alcohol in it but it's streak-free, even if you're a bit lacking in the elbow grease department when it comes to the buffing up! Scrunch up a couple of pages of newspaper and use to wipe clean.

Baths and Showers

- Use a solution of half vinegar and half water to get rid of limescale, particularly on heavily encrusted taps, and to polish up the tiles. (This method isn't suitable for plated taps of any kind, especially gold.) For heavy caking, soak paper towels, wrap around the tap in a plastic bag held in place with an elastic band and leave overnight. Remove in the morning and the limescale comes clean away.
- For stubborn marks on the bath try toothpaste rubbed on with a cloth; the slight abrasive action should shift them. And don't forget those old toothbrushes – they're ideal for scrubbing hard-to-get-at areas around the taps.
- Enamel baths – use bicarbonate of soda rubbed on with a damp

cloth. Give it a good rinse to get rid of the powdery residue, buff with
a dry cloth and it should come up sparkly white as new.

♦ If the enamel has worn off you may need to redo it – a great tip is to
use white car paint.

♦ Another easy and cheap way of cleaning the bath is to fill it with warm
water and add a mug full of cheap biological washing powder. Leave to
soak for a few hours or even overnight, empty and clean with a cloth.

♦ For glass shower screens, use lemon juice diluted in water in an old
squirty bottle after every shower, and rub over with a flannel.

♦ To de-scale the shower head – soak in white vinegar (if it's plastic) for
a couple hours, and rinse thoroughly. And for limescale in the shower
spray on a mix of washing soda and vinegar. Limescale lurks in the
sliding door bits of the shower too, so once you get that off treat the
tracks with Vaseline.

Mildew and Muck

♦ After using your chosen form of bathroom cleaning solution, follow
up with a 'whitening toothpaste' (one with sodium bicarbonate in) –
or even a paste of bicarbonate of soda and water – applied with an
old toothbrush to the grout and window putty. Leave for five minutes
and rinse off, or you can use thick bleach applied with a toothbrush.

♦ For gunky roller blinds, take them down, unroll and put the material
into the bath along with biological washing powder for a long soak.
Scrub gently with a soft nail brush. It might even be possible to undo
the whole thing and stick the material part in the machine but do
check that's okay as some Old-Stylers have come unstuck (literally!)
when the material curled up when wet.

Polish up those Bathroom Tiles

◆ Get out the car cleaning wax and polish up your bathroom tiles so the water just runs off after every shower. Buff it up with a pair of old jeans, cut and hemmed into rags.

Toilet Training

Dreaded limescale round the top of the loo?

◆ Soak wads of toilet paper in vinegar and pad it round the rim. It keeps the vinegar where it's needed and only needs a tiny bit of elbow grease afterwards.

◆ Add a couple of denture cleaning tablets to the bowl and leave overnight. Cheap 'value' tablets are just as good as the branded ones.

Smelly toilet?

◆ Avoid blockages and neutralise toilet odours by pouring a cup of bicarbonate of soda into the pan once a week. Or even throw some soda crystals down the loo before bedtime and flush away in the morning.

◆ If a limescale blitz treatment is needed, mix up 2 tablespoons of baking soda, 2 tablespoons of white vinegar, 2 cups of water and 2 teaspoons of tea tree oil, leave for an hour and put into an old spray container before spraying on the limescale.

Prevention is Better than Cure . . .

Top tips to save on scrubbing time in the future:

◆ *Economy bubble bath in an old washing-up bottle squirted around the bath will clean it up well after each use, and an old squash bottle is useful for rinsing. Give it a quick wipe down right after a bath or shower as the steam will keep it moist. Don't forget to clean the plug. Turpentine works well on rubber stoppers.*

◆ *Liquid soap is more hygienic and saves scummy mess round the sink which means you've less to clean.*

◆ *If you've got a soap dish, rub cooking or baby oil on the bottom to stop the soap sticking to it.*

◆ *Clean your basin every day, removing soap scum, limescale and germs.*

◆ *Paint the bottom of metal shaving-foam cans with a little clear nail varnish to stop them leaving rusty ring marks.*

◆ *Gloopy toothbrush mugs are a haven for bacteria. Pop in the dishwasher once a week.*

◆ *Once a week chuck some bicarb down the plughole along with a dash of lemon juice to keep the pipe work smelling sweet. And don't waste new bicarb on the job; use the stuff that's been kicking around in the back of your fridge keeping it odour-free.*

◆ *Last thing at night throw some leftover, flat or just plain cheap value cola down the toilets and round the sinks. They'll come up sparkling and it will probably put you off the stuff for life – if that's what it does to your bathroom, what does it do to your insides?*

The Grotty Jobs

Okay, let's be honest. Nobody enjoys unblocking the sink, trying to clean baby sick out of the carpet or the stress of trying to get kids' felt tip pen out of the sofa – but where there's a few home ingredients there's a way...

Blocked Sink

◆   *Chuck a handful of bicarb of soda down the drain followed by a cup of vinegar. Wait a couple of hours then pour a kettle of boiling water down there.*

◆   *For more serious blockages, gently lower a hook down the hole (like the end of a coat hanger) and pull it up. You're likely to get lovely clumps of hair and gunk out and it's a pretty revolting job – not one to do first thing in the morning or after your Sunday lunch, though some Old-Stylers claim it's a strangely satisfying experience...?*

BBQ Cleaning

This ranks high on the list of horrid jobs so stick your grill pans in the bath with lots of hot water and some soda crystals, leave to soak for a couple of hours and the grease should wipe off easily. Biological washing powder works in the same way – remember, value stuff is okay. And if you don't fancy hogging the bath for a few hours, bundle the grill pan along with your cleaning liquid into a bin liner and sit it outside in the sun for a few hours.

Common Stains and How to Get Rid of Them

Blood on Mattress

An old army wives' trick is to make a paste with bleach and talcum powder. Rub it gently into the mattress surface. The bleach removes the blood and the talc absorbs the bleach so it doesn't sink straight in. It works a treat but you'll need to use enough talcum powder to make a very thick paste, one that's spreadable rather than pourable. As the talc dries it draws the bleach and the blood away from the mattress. As soon as the talc is reasonably dry, vacuum it off the mattress – you may end up with a slightly lighter patch but it's a lot better than a blood stain!

Brown Stains down the Loo

For light-brown stains on the back of the bowl (a build-up of limescale over the years) squeeze vinegar up under the rim and scrub with an old toothbrush. Do this once a week till it's clear and then chuck some old flat or value cola down the loo on a regular basis to keep it clean and sparkly.

Burnt Pans

Boiling water with either salt or washing powder in it left to stand for a couple of hours should do the trick, or boil up some cola.

Crayon Marks on Walls

Remove with toothpaste rather than spending on cream cleaners like 'Cif'.

Crystal Glasses with Stains
Fill with white vinegar and warm water, leave for a couple of hours (or as long as you can) before washing the glasses.

Dull Chrome Appliances
Rub on white vinegar with a paper towel. Leave for a few hours then rinse.

Fingerprints on Walls
Strange but true – use a piece of white bread to dab away finger marks.

Make-up Stains on the Carpet
Wash with warm soapy water then soak up the water with talc, leave to dry and vacuum up. Or try good old bicarb – wet the carpet and then sprinkle the bicarb on it and rub with a sponge. You might have to repeat it but it should do the job.

Lipstick on the Carpet
Use talcum powder or cornflour – pour lots onto the stain, work it into the pile of the carpet and leave overnight.

Gravy Splatters on the Carpet
Rub over some washing-up liquid as soon as possible to start breaking it down, rinse and leave to dry.

Hair Dye on Bath Sealant
Try painting on thick bleach with a toothbrush, leave it till the sealant turns white and rinse off.

Limescale on Taps
Rub with half a lemon, leave for a few minutes and rinse. Or soak cotton wool pads or paper towels in a half-vinegar/half-water solution and drape round the build-up – leave overnight and limescale should come away easily.

Marks on Vinyl Floors
Rub a little silver polish wadding over the mark, let it dry and wipe away.

Nicotine Stains on China
Get out the denture-cleaning tablets – the supermarket value version. Put the ornament in a plastic jug. You'll probably need two or more denture tablets and hand-hot water and leave to soak overnight.

Olive Oil on the Carpet
Use lots of kitchen towel to blot up the excess oil then put salt on the stain and brush it after it's soaked up the last of the oil. Dissolve some washing soda in hot water and dab it on, going from the outside in so the stain doesn't spread. If that still leaves marks, use fly spray on the stain, holding the can about 4 inches away, and then rub off.

Pet Litter Trays
Soak in vinegar and water to get rid of the grey litter mess stuck to the bottom. Two days later you can rinse it out as good as new.

Poo Stains on Nappies
Good old-fashioned sunlight can do the trick, as hanging washable nappies (after washing!) on the line in bright sunlight fades the stains.

Red Wine Stains
Rumour has it the Queen uses soda water and blotting paper for her red wine stains — and she's got the right idea. You need to blot away as much as you can, though you can use a clean cloth or kitchen towel. Rinse with cold water, then use carpet shampoo or wash clothing as normal. For red wine stains in decanters add a few grains of rice and some white vinegar. Swirl around gently; the abrasive action of the rice will gently remove inaccessible deposits.

Scuff Marks on Laminate Floor
Try a pencil eraser. For those that don't budge, go over with a colour-matched felt tip pen — yes, you're allowed to pinch one from the kids' room! For ink stains on lino, try fly spray, hair spray or even milk.

Soot on Carpets
Sprinkle the mark with salt, leave for half an hour, vacuum up and shampoo the carpet.

Spilt Milk
Leave talcum powder on the stain for 24 hours and then vacuum up.

REAL OLD-STYLE STORY

**I'm a cabbie and if milk leaked out from bags of shopping
I always used to spray our seats with aftershave.
My husband would be cross if I pinched his 'posh'
stuff but 'Denim' used to work a treat!**

Stainless Steel Appliances
Wipe with a little baby oil on a clean rag – brings them up a treat.

Stickers on Doors and Skirting Boards
Pull off the paper surface and spray the sticky residue with WD40, soak
and wipe away.

Tea-stained Mugs
Put a mix of denture tablets and water in each and leave to soak
overnight or use washing powder and boiling water. Or dip a damp
cloth in a bit of bicarb of soda and wipe it round the cup. Even half a
lemon is pretty good – squeeze a bit of the juice into the mug, then
rub the lemon all around the inside of the mug and leave overnight.

Vases
To de-gunk and get rid of water marks use denture tablets left in water,
or baby sterilising tablets – even a bit of rice with vinegar – and shake
up and leave for a couple of hours.

Walls

For grubby stains, such as fingerprints or crayons, or just general wear and tear, scrub with a mild sugar soap solution, but make sure you test an area first if you've got fancy wallpaper.

Watermarks on Woodwork

Buff up with a brazil nut (not with the shell on!) or rub shoe polish into the mark.

Wax Stains on Carpets

Put kitchen roll over the wax and use an iron (not set too high) to melt it, allowing the kitchen roll to soak it up. Other Old-Stylers have used brown paper and an iron, which works just as well. Scrape off as much as you can, pour a little boiling water over the wax that's left and mop it up, dabbing, not rubbing, with a towel or something similar as you go. And if you don't want to 'iron' your carpet, a hot water bottle will do just as well.

How to Banish Nasty Smells

We spend over £300 million a year on air fresheners and scented candles to keep our homes smelling sweet – but you can save some cash by freshening up the Old-Style way.

For general whiffs and unpleasant smells, put bowls of vinegar around the room and leave for a couple of days till all the smells have gone. If the smell's got into the curtains, spray with a solution of two-thirds water and one-third white vinegar. For stale cupboards or fridges, a pot of bicarb stored open at the back works a treat. You can leave a lemon in there too but not for long as it'll go mouldy!

Smelly Bins
Get a cheap throwaway cloth and put some lavender oil on it. Put the cloth in a bag in the bin, and when the bin's opened all you'll smell is lavender. When the smell gives out, just add some more oil or change the cloth. Or just leave some bicarb in the bottom of the bin. Clean out the bin with water and tea tree oil to get rid of lingering smells.

Fishy Smells
Cook up fish for tea and you risk smelling it for weeks afterwards – a quick solution is to boil up some water in a pan with lemon quarters.

Onion Smells
What about onion smells on your hands? You can buy 'steel soap', which is basically a lump of stainless steel, but Old-Stylers have found their own thrifty ways including rubbing their hands on the bottom of the sink or on something metal like a ladle.

Smelly Cat Tray
Baking soda at the bottom of the cat tray helps with the smell of urine – try it at the bottom of the bin too. And for children's wee, sprinkle bicarb into the carpet in the baby's room, just as you would with Shake 'n' Vac and then vacuum up.

Smelly Thermos Flasks and Lunch Boxes

Use boiling water with lemon juice in vacuum flasks and leave, or use water with denture tablets but rinse well afterwards. And for whiffy plastic lunch boxes or containers, try scrunched-up newspaper rolled into balls and left inside overnight to take smells out – it even gets rid of the smell of garlic sausage!

Smelly Salad Drawer

Try lining the bottom of your veggie or salad drawer with old newspaper to absorb the smells and soak up any moisture, keeping veg and salad fresh for longer.

Sick Smells

A large tablespoon of bicarb in about a pint of water should do it. It won't stain as the liquid will be clear but you may get a powdery residue when it dries which you can just vaccuum up.

MAKE YOUR OWN OLD-STYLE GEL AIR FRESHENER

You will need:

450ml (16fl oz) distilled water
Essential oil/fragrance of your choice
1 packet of gelatine
Food colouring (optional)

◆ Heat half the water almost to boiling. Add the gelatine and stir until dissolved.
◆ Remove from the heat and add the remaining water, 10–20 drops of oil or fragrance and the food colouring if desired.
◆ Pour the mixture into clean baby-food jars and set at room temperature overnight.

You can put the jars in the fridge if you need them to set more quickly, but be aware that the smell will permeate the fridge. And the cost saving? Well, it works out at about 12 pence for a 'Glade'-sized jar. You can also buy little shot glasses very cheaply – try the local pound shop.

Chapter 2

SHOPPING
What to Buy
and How to Reuse It

Shopping has become the number-one pastime in this country. Take any typical Sunday afternoon; for most people it's a toss-up between IKEA or Tesco. But why do we go shopping so much? Is it because we're bored? Got money burning a hole in our pockets? Or do we just get a kick from a dose of the old 'retail therapy'?

Instead of amassing a load of stuff you don't need or want, take a look at what you're actually buying – once the initial buzz of buying it has faded – and whether you really *need* it.

This chapter's about learning to shop the Old-Style way, and making everything go that little bit further. So it looks at ways to reuse stuff you'd usually chuck straight in the bin, and how to get a second life from pretty much everything. Plus home-made beauty treatments, how to save a fortune on your creams, potions and fancy salon prices and how to bring up baby the Old-Style way.

NEW-STYLE SHOPPING SOLUTIONS

Before trying out the Old-Style tricks, it's important to tackle your own spending impulses. To help, here's a brief extract from my book *The Money Diet* on beating your impulses.

RETAIL THERAPY AT A PRICE YOU CAN AFFORD (COURTESY OF *THE MONEY DIET*)

Fight the Impulse!

When you shop, it's not what you need that's the problem, but the things you don't need; it's when the 'gotta have' impulse rises from your belly and a lust for spending springs from your loins. The child inside says, 'I want, I want, I want,' and once that little voice is heard, it's virtually impossible to stop.

Martin's Money Mantras

I've a couple of easy-to-remember mantras for you to chant to yourself when you are about to spend. One for those who are short of cash, and therefore need to be long on self-discipline, and one for those who can, within reason, buy pretty much whatever they want.

> **MARTIN'S MONEY MANTRA 1 – FOR THE SKINT**
> Do I need it? Can I afford it? Have I checked if it's cheaper anywhere else? If an answer is 'No' or 'Don't know' – STOP!

Quite simply, if the answer to any of these questions is 'No', don't buy it. If you don't need it, don't buy it. If you can't afford it, don't buy it. If you haven't checked whether it's cheaper anywhere else, don't buy it.

> **MARTIN'S MONEY MANTRA 2 – FOR EVERYONE ELSE**
> **Will I use it? Is it worth it? Have I checked if it's cheaper**
> **anywhere else? If an answer is 'No' or 'Don't know' – STOP!**

This may sound just a little harsh – after all, you can afford it. But the funny thing is, sometimes we make purchases purely out of desire, yet get no real benefit apart from the pure shopping buzz. Are you really willing to shell out for that buzz? So ask: 'Will I use it?' If not, don't buy it. 'Is it worth it?' Even if you will use it, will you use it enough to justify the cash? If not, don't buy it. In economic terms, this is known as 'opportunity cost'. What else could you do with the money, and would you enjoy that more? Take a look at your wardrobe, book shelves, shoe rack and CD collection – are there clothes or shoes hardly ever or never worn, unread books and unlistened-to CDs? With this Money Mantra you may spend the cash on something else instead, and gain more fun or benefit.

Finally, have you checked if it's available cheaper anywhere else? If you haven't, spare a little time to do so, especially with a big purchase. The savings could be huge, leaving more money in your pocket for other things.

Remember the mantra that's appropriate to you, and as you are about to take 'it' to the till, repeat it to yourself.

Sometimes Time is Money

Now don't think I'm being a complete party-pooper here. I realise that at certain times money mantras are unrealistic, for those who aren't skint anyway. To quote the old cliché, time is money – and when you're in a rush, buying quickly can be cheaper than buying cheaply.

For example, if you're holding a party and need new music, I would of course suggest using a shopping robot on the Internet, such as Kelkoo or pricerunner, to find the cheapest prices, then trying cashback sites and three or four high-street stores to ensure you're getting the best deal. Yet if the party is tonight, and you're rushing home to prepare food, getting the CDs in the first shop may be the MoneySaving move – if it means you can use public transport instead of a taxi; you have more time to cook so food isn't wasted; or you've more time to shop for a good deal on booze and snacks. All of these are valid reasons.

Danger! Sales!

Sales are wonderful for MoneySavers, but they also hold a measure of danger. Bagging a discount doesn't automatically mean you're saving money. In the panicked, fevered rush to grab sales bargains, it's easy to buy lots of things you don't really need. A suit reduced by 50 per cent is a great deal, but a bad buy if it's never worn. As I'm neither stupid nor brave enough to bring up shopping gender differences, I thought I would reprint a joke floating round the Internet:

> 'A man will pay £2 for a £1 item he needs.
> A woman will pay £1 for a £2 item she doesn't need.'

Things often look different outside the sales than in. And you have no right to return goods simply because you don't like them. Shops often grant us this privilege but withhold it in the sales. That's why when sales shopping, it's even more important to shop smart, because you can't change your mind.

LEARNING TO SHOP THE OLD-STYLE WAY

Think of this as a re-education. Like any learning process, don't expect to 'do' Old-Style in one easy go, just as you wouldn't expect to pass an exam after just a few days in school. Instead of trying to do it all at once it's a good idea to pick out one or two things that catch your eye and make you think 'Yes! I can do that!' Do them until they become second nature before picking out another thing (or two) to do.

Old-Style taking New-Style's 'Can I find it cheaper anywhere else?' and morphing it into 'Can I find a cheaper way?' Old-Style is about being thrifty and not wasting money when there's an easier or cheaper alternative, and not randomly chucking any old thing in your shopping basket as you tour the supermarket aisles. It's about budgeting and asking yourself whether you really need what you're buying or just 'want' it.

And Old-Style is of course about making everything go that little bit further, so we're talking recycling and how to save money by finding a second use for everything before it hits either the bin or the recycling tip.

Even on a small scale, for example, instead of chucking away leftovers after a meal, freeze what's left. It can be used for another meal or to reheat as a quick snack one night when you're tight for time.

So before you part with your cash, the number-one rule is always to ask yourself whether there's a cheaper way of getting it, borrowing it, making it or whatever, rather than buying it.

Use up things before buying more. Okay, if there's a great BOGOF (buy one get one free) deal you might stock up, but buying and opening new packets of cereal, jars of jam, packets of biscuits or whatever before you've finished the last one just doesn't make good Old-Style sense.

And every now and then have a 'use up' month when you don't buy or open anything new until you've used up something, whether it's an old bottle of half-used shampoo, a jar of coffee or packet of cereal. It clears your cupboards and saves money.

The Downshift Challenge – Courtesy of Martin's *The Money Diet* Book

Don't worry, I'm not about to tell you to always buy 'no-frills'. Yet I want to challenge you to try to downshift. Quality is worthwhile and can justify expense, but are you really getting it? To check, slip out of your shopping habits and occasionally try something one level cheaper. Sometimes you'll like it, sometimes you won't. For me, I don't notice the difference between no-frills and supermarket own-brand baked beans – yet I'd never dream of drinking no-frills diet cola, nor would I wipe my bottom with ultra-cheap toilet roll.

This is about finding what fits and costs less. Next time you want tinned spaghetti, get four of your normal, one supermarket own-brand and one no-frills and try them out. Downshift savings can be huge – take a look at this sample from different shops on the same day.

Bread 800g Loaf
Kingsmill 83p each
Supermarket own-brand 69p
Supermarket no-frills brand 28p

Long Grain Rice 1kg
Uncle Ben's £2.15
Supermarket own-brand 82p
Supermarket no-frills brand 55p

London Hair Cut
Vidal Sassoon £42
Toni and Guy Essensuals £39
Fish £27
Mr Toppers £6

Tea 0.25kg
PG Tips £1.88
Supermarket own-brand £1.25
Supermarket no-frills brand 49p

Skin Lotion
Vaseline £2.90 (200ml)
Nivea £2.99 (250ml)
Pharmacy own-brand £1.59 (250ml)

Sunglasses
FCUK £56
Boots Dial 45s £20
Boots Fixed Tint £10
Superdrug Fashion Tint £3.99

Take just one of the above examples. If you used one packet of rice a week, over a year Uncle Ben's would cost £112, the supermarket own-brand £42 and the no-frills brand £28. Are you really sure the extra £70 or even £80 is worth it? Try the downshift challenge to see.

It Works in Practice
For an ITV programme I challenged a family to downshift. I followed them in the supermarket, mimicking their weekly shopping, just choosing one brand level lower.

Their trolley came to £130. Mine was £85, a third cheaper, roughly what I'd expect. For the next week they lived off my trolley and, to their surprise, only noticed the difference for half the stuff. Where they didn't see a difference, they switched, and their new weekly shop became £105 – a reduction of £1,300 a year without noticing a difference.

Proof that Sometimes There's no Difference at All

Own-brands are often made in the same factories, with the same ingredients, as main brands. No-frills brands are sometimes identical too, the only difference being the box and brand. Of course, no company will confirm this, so I put out a request via the website called 'The Great Own-brand Hunt', asking anyone who'd worked in a factory to dish the dirt. Hundreds responded, admitting products as varied as cereals and DVD players were all the same thing.

Have a look below to see a sample and you'll be surprised. There's still no way of knowing whether these are or ever were correct but it's (unbranded) food for thought.

Don't be conned. Try the downshift challenge and open your mind.

Manufacturer	Product	Rumoured to be sold as
McVities'	Digestive biscuits	Tesco, Asda, Sainsbury's, M&S, Aldi, Lidl, Happy Shopper
Chanel	Make-up	Bourjois
Sony	Electrical goods	Aiwa
Papermill Direct	Printer paper	Epson, HP
Johnsons	Baby wipes	Tesco
French Connection	Clothing	House of Fraser 'Linea', Great Plains
Highland Spring	Mineral water	Tesco
Crown	Paint	Do It All
Buitoni	Pasta	Tesco, Asda
Triton	Showers	Wickes

Here are just a few Old-Style ways to save money with little or no effort at all:

◆ *When you cook a meal, make an extra portion and freeze it so when you're feeling lazy and in danger of resorting to a takeaway there's something yummy already in the freezer.*

◆ *Reuse bread and sandwich bags or the paper bags that come with fruit.*

◆ *Why make the effort to cook a big 'meal' every night? Have something 'on toast' once a week.*

◆ *Always check out the little 'yellow sticker' reduction sections in supermarkets or shop near to closing time for last-minute bargains, particularly on the deli counter.*

◆ *Make your own lunches, sandwiches or salads. These can be made very cheaply at home compared with spending around £5 a day at a posh sandwich shop like Pret à Manger or M&S.*

The Grocery Challenge

This is a monthly challenge on the Old-Style chat boards. You're not competing against everyone else but against yourself so there's no winners or losers. The idea is to try and shave as much as you can off your monthly food budget every month.

The Grocery Challenge is much more about shopping wisely and thriftily than it is about 'spending less money'. As you learn the Old-Style tricks of the trade, so to speak, you'll probably find out you're actually eating better for less!

We waste around £420 a year on food – all those bits and pieces of fruit and veg that go off before you use them, yoghurts you don't get around to eating before the best-before date, bread that's gone mouldy and milk that's gone off. It all adds up so time to rethink your shopping style. Instead of a haphazard rush round the supermarket, randomly grabbing anything that takes your fancy, plan your meals, write a list and shop from that list so there's nothing left to hit the bin come the end of the week.

Meal planning, careful budgeting, cooking from scratch, batch cooking and freezing are all great ways to start. And where do you shop? While M&S might be truly gorgeous, it's expensive compared with other outlets so try shopping in Lidl, Aldi, Netto or buying the Tesco 'value' range.

And of course you don't have to use the supermarkets at all. In general, popping out to your local shops every day can prove more expensive than doing one large supermarket shop, but if you're limited by what you can carry as you're walking, cycling or going by bus then chances are you won't overstock or overspend. So, for some, a daily shop may be a good Old-Style way, reminiscent of the days before many households had freezers and fridges and you popped out for your daily loaf of fresh bread, nipped in the local butcher and got your fruit and veg fresh from the greengrocer.

How to Do the Grocery Challenge

In a nutshell, the idea is working out ways to save money on your food bill each week, simple as that. Most people don't have a clue how much the 'average' weekly shop costs. Some weeks it's more if you've got people round; other weeks you're away so it's less, so first time round you'll probably have to take an educated guess.

Save Your Receipts

Save all your receipts for a month. Yes, that does include the ones from the local shop when you ran out of milk or had to nip out and buy something for the kids' packed lunch at the last minute!

At the end of the month work out how much you've spent; then see what you've bought that you don't need (any wastage and treats) and take that off the amount. Use that as your total to aim for next month and each month try and shave off as much as you think you can, whether it's £1 or £20 a week.

If you're currently spending £200 a month, don't suddenly drop to £100 – you'll never do it – but if you cut £20 a month off for a few months you'll get there eventually without feeling you're missing out, and you won't get disheartened halfway through and give up. You might think you've done everything you can in the first month but there are loads of new ideas here and on the Old-Style boards and you'll often find you can save a bit more one way or another.

Write a Menu Plan

Okay, time to write your shopping list. First up, look in the cupboards, fridge and freezer to see what you've got and what you can make with it rather than just buying the same old stuff week in, week out.

◆   *Organise your cupboards. If it's all chucked in there in a huge heap you'll never find anything and end up buying a load more stuff when you've got enough for a few meals already.*

◆   *Check for out-of-date stuff once in a while, though ideally use it up before it goes off.*

◆ *If you're stumped for what to make from the contents of your fridge and store cupboard, check out www.cookingbynumbers.com – type in the ingredients and it comes up with a list of recipes.*

◆ *With a meal plan you'll be able to use up everything fresh, and you won't end up chucking away food you've forgotten to use, never got around to eating or just don't know what to do with.*

There are loads of recipe ideas on the Old-Style boards but all you need to do is work out what you're going to eat every day and the ingredients you'll need. Then shop from the list rather than randomly grabbing stuff off the supermarket shelf. A good approach is always, 'Here's what I have in the cupboard, what can I make?' A good basic shopping list should include your menu-planning ingredients along with any BOGOFs or items nearing the end of their shelf life. Working from your favourite recipes, you'll then see the type of foods you do eat, and can start building your basic store cupboard around that. There's loads more information on how to build a basic store cupboard, together with recipe ideas, in Chapter 8.

As a general rule, start by basing your meals around staples like rice, pasta, potatoes and noodles as these are very cheap, filling and healthy. Make a list of how many meals you can make with these as the main ingredient, such as pasta with home-made sauce (made from tinned tomatoes or tinned sweetcorn and tuna), cheesy potato pie, rice with vegetables, jacket potatoes, macaroni cheese . . . the list goes on!

Check out the menu plans section on the Old-Style boards, ideas for kids' packed lunches, how to eat for less than £20 a week and organising your recipes so you're not left with half-used tins or bits of veg kicking about.

The £15 Meal Plan

Here's just one example of the number of meals one Old-Styler made with £15!

◆ 8 portions of cannelloni: 4 filled with ricotta cheese (sort of Italian cottage cheese) and courgettes and 4 filled with white sauce and tomato sauce and mince

◆ 2 loaves of bread

◆ 6 rolls

◆ 8 sweetcorn and potato fritters

◆ 1 cake (8 portions)

◆ 1 spaghetti with courgettes and cream omelette (8 portions)

◆ 6 portions of turkey and mozzarella balls

◆ 2 portions of potato mash

◆ 1 pizza with courgettes

◆ 1 pizza with potatoes

◆ 2 portions of small cherry tomatoes with stuffing and mozzarella cheese

◆ 4 portions of potato gnocchi (dumplings)

◆ 6 portions of potatoes, mushrooms and Emmental cheese bake

◆ 8 crêpes

◆ 1 portion of chicken breast in white wine with sweetcorn

◆ 2 portions of mince and potatoes

Go Shopping

It's all about balance. If there's one product you love – say expensive cooking oils – and you're miserable switching to the value ones then cut back on other areas and still use the extra-virgin olive oil that you love. Old-Style isn't about making yourself miserable; it's about finding out what works for you.

With fruit and veg, beware of buying the bigger value packs if you won't use it all. It's better to work out how much you will need and buy them loosely in a bag, even if it's just one onion and a couple of carrots. **All the processed foods in the freezers like chicken burgers and pizzas generally work out much more expensive than if you cook them from scratch, and doing so is far healthier.** Here are a few really cheap meals that can be made in minutes. For more recipe ideas, see Chapter 8.

CHEESY POTATO PIE

This is made with a few potatoes from a bag of Tesco white potatoes (just under 90p for a big bag). Boil and mash the spuds with a little milk and butter, put in an ovenproof dish with grated cheese on and grill till cheese melts. Serve with tinned spaghetti, which you can pick up for around 10p a tin if you go for Tesco value ones.

SAUSAGE CASSEROLE

Use a Coleman's sauce mix for this (around 60p) and add Tesco value thin sausages. Serve with mash and veg, which can be a bag of frozen veg or value peas.

HOME-MADE PIZZA

Make the base from a simple scone mix, bung on some tomato purée and your favourite toppings and bake. You could also use 'value' pitta breads for the base.

Old-Style Grocery Shopping Tips

◆ *If you pop into the supermarket for just a few items, take a basket rather than a trolley. That way you can't carry too much extra to the till.*

◆ *Only go to the aisles on your list. Don't wander or you'll spend more time and money!*

◆ *Only buy BOGOFs that you actually use or are on your shopping list, otherwise they're not the bargain they seem to be and you should stay away!*

◆ *Shop late at night or just before closing for the best bargains and to snap up the reduced fresh deli produce.*

◆ *Bulk-buy milk and bread for the freezer.*

Shop Online

So you've done your list, know what you want but it means going on a Friday afternoon with the kids and risking succumbing to 'pester power' for sweets and treats or doing it Friday night after work when you're starving hungry. Think about shopping online once a month. Yes, you do pay currently for some services like Tesco, Sainsbury's and Asda, but you can often get lots of deals like £5 off for recommending a friend. Or find out if one of the neighbours is up for splitting the cost, do the one order online and split the delivery charge – if you go for the early part of the week, Tesco delivery is cheaper than weekends, and if it saves you buying a load of extra stuff you don't need then it's worth it.

Make Everything Go Further . . .

◆ Snap dishwasher tablets in half to use (unless it's a really dirty load).

◆ Water down shampoo, liquid soap, shower gel, fabric conditioner etc.

◆ Mix 'value' products with more expensive stuff – like washing powder.

◆ Use scissors for cutting open toothpaste tubes so you use every last drop – there's always loads left in the nozzle at the end.

◆ Stand 'empty' bottles upside down overnight to get the last dregs of salad cream, tomato ketchup or shampoo out.

◆ Swill out cooking sauce jars with a little water or milk to use the lot and make the sauce go further.

◆ Turn stale bread into breadcrumbs and freeze to bulk out meat-balls, burgers and meatloaf.

REUSE: RECYCLING STARTS AT HOME

We chuck away one tonne of rubbish each year per household. We all know we should reuse more but dropping off your empty bottles, cardboard boxes or clothing takes time and effort, and a special trip out can be a false economy. Websites like www.recycle-more.co.uk have loads of info on what you can recycle and where your nearest facility is, or try www.recyclenow.com

But before you hit the recycle banks start by reusing things, as recycling begins at home.

Hang On To It!

Before you bin it, can you use it again?

- ◆ *Hang on to tubes of unused glue that come with flatpack furniture – great for cutting and sticking afternoons with the kids.*
- ◆ *Make the most of those free pens from Argos or any that come through the door with the junk mail.*
- ◆ *Shower caps that come free in hotel rooms are great for wrapping round shoes when you're packing suitcases.*
- ◆ *Keep plastic cutlery (M&S is great quality unlike some of the cheap disposable cutlery) – handy for picnics out.*

Reusing Round the House

- ◆ *Save supermarket plastic carrier bags to reuse as bin liners. They've got handles so they're easy to tie up to throw away. Okay, so you won't save megabucks but they're often thicker than the ones you can buy and you're helping the environment.*

- Cut the tops off large milk and orange juice containers and use the bases for plants or as watering cans for hanging baskets, even mini cloches to protect small outdoor plants.
- Margarine tubs make great freezer containers for sauces and leftovers, and the plastic tubs from Costco are good too.
- Cut open old tea bags and pour the tea into the soil around pot plants – it's got nutritional qualities for the soil (apparently) and saves on plant food.
- Save small screw-top jars like mustard jars to store fuses, screws, nuts and bolts to save them rattling round in drawers and cupboards.
- Reuse cardboard from cereal packets as postcards when you're entering competitions or sending off for offers.
- Old baked bean tins with the labels soaked off and decorated make funky pencil holders for the kids.

Reuse Junk Mail

- Reuse envelopes and the back of letters for scrap paper and lists.
- Save any wrapping like bubble wrap, polystyrene chips and padded envelopes – great when you're sending out presents or packaging up your eBay sales.
- Cut out the bits with your name and address and use as pre-addressed labels.

Reuse for Cash

◆ *Aluminium cans – you can get around 1p back for each one – check out www.thinkcans.com for your nearest recycling depot.*

◆ *Take good-quality clothes that you don't wear or that don't fit to nearby dress agencies. You can find them in the local phone book and you'll get a cut of the profits when sold.*

◆ *Got an old tea set or dinner service you don't use, need or want? Sell it to www.lostpottery.co.uk who source replacement china and discontinued lines.*

◆ *Get your old printer cartridges refilled rather than buy new; saves up to 60 per cent on the cost of a new one and helps the environment. There are masses of websites doing this and packs are stocked in many computer and stationery shops.*

What Else Can Be Reused?

Christmas Cards
Tesco and WH Smith usually have bins outside stores every year after Christmas – all proceeds go to the Woodland Trust www.woodland-trust.org.uk. Or turn old cards into gift tags or decorations. See Chapter 7 for more great ideas.

Glasses
Hand specs in to your local optician who can forward them to Vision Aid: www.vao.org.uk

Paint
www.communityrepaint.org.uk – don't chuck it as it contains solvents that shouldn't be tipped down the drain. Donate full or part-used tins.

Books
Try www.greenmetropolis.com for paperbacks – you'll get £3 for every book sold and a donation is made to the Woodland Trust. Alternatively, flog them on eBay or Amazon.

Mobile Phones
There are around 90 million redundant mobile phones lying in cupboards and drawers. As well as putting them on eBay, there are a number of companies who will pay to take them off your hands. See www.moneysavingexpert.com/mobilerecycling for the current best payers.

Oil
Never ever tip this stuff down the sink or drain. Even local tips have a special section for used engine oil. To find your nearest oil bank go to www.oilbankline.co.uk

Tools
Tools for Self Reliance (www.tfsr.org) is a charity that sends tools to places like Africa – check their site for a list of tools they currently need but sewing machines, carpentry tools, bike repair tools and industrial power tools are always needed.

Swap Your Stuff

Anyone of a certain age who remembers Keith Chegwin swapping kids' unwanted toys and Christmas presents on *Multi Coloured Swap Shop* will be up for this. You can swap unwanted items at www.freecycle.org – no money changes hands, it's an American idea that's now over here and all you do is sign up to your local network and receive regular emails telling you what's available.

De-Clutter the Easy Way

But what if you're the sort of person who just hoards everything because you're worried about getting rid of it or think it's wasteful to chuck it out? Set yourself a target to chuck or reuse something every day and work your way round the house. So, in the kitchen for example, you could take that bag of old newspapers to the nearest recycle depot when you're next out, chuck that dead houseplant, decide that you're really never going to use that old and useless kitchen appliance so put aside for a car boot sale or selling on eBay... you get the gist. The danger with hoarding too much stuff is that you'll probably end up buying more when you've already got perfectly good items lying around the house that you could use if you could only find them!

And once you've streamlined and de-cluttered your house, make it a rule that every time you buy something new you get rid of something old. So if you've bought a new set of mugs because the others are chipped and cracked, get rid of them or, better still, use them as plant pots.

The Big Stuff

Here's how to get rid of big stuff without paying the council to take it away or dumping it at the local tip:

Bikes: www.re-cycle.org needs second-hand bicycles and parts to donate to the developing world.

Furniture: try www.gumtree.com or offer to your local Salvation Army or charity groups. Saves paying the council to take it away if you can't sell it.

Computers: www.computersforcharity.org.uk – free UK collection and they can be reused for schools, charities and voluntary groups. Or try www.free-computers.org

OLD-STYLE BEAUTY TREATMENTS

Believe the adverts and you'll spend a small fortune on creams, potions and designer-named skincare – but many of the ingredients in your kitchen cupboard can often double up when it comes to bathtime beauty.

Bathtime

◆ If you run out of bubble bath, stick a squirt of shampoo or
   conditioner into your bath water. Great for using up shampoos you're
   not keen on or have been given as presents.

◆ Run out of shaving foam? Use conditioner as it softens the hairs
   before shaving.

◆ Mix a bit of fake tan with moisturiser for your face. Makes your fake
   tan last longer and you won't end up orange if you've been too
   heavy-handed!

◆ Every now and then have a 'use-up' month (as you would in your
   kitchen cupboards) where you don't buy anything new till you've used
   up the last dregs from shampoo bottles, moisturiser or bars of soap.

Make it Go that Bit Further

◆ Most products are dual purpose – out-of-date sun cream can be
   reused as body moisturiser (unless it's the really thick factor 500 white
   stuff).

◆ Apply hand cream before sticking your rubber gloves on to do the
   washing up. The heat helps the cream to soak in super fast. Even if
   you forget the hand cream always use your marigolds to protect your
   hands. That way you'll need to buy less of the stuff in the first place!

REAL OLD-STYLE STORY

My Charles Worthington shampoo proved to be an unlikely toilet cleaner! My three-year-old lobbed half the bottle down the toilet and watched it bubble up as he flushed it away! Noooooooo!

Go Home-made

- *For a wonderful hand moisturiser, mix together 1 tablespoon of olive oil and 1 tablespoon of sugar, massage into your hands, leave for two minutes and then rinse off – leaves hands super-soft. Great for tired feet too!*
- *For super-white nail tips soak your fingers in lemon juice for 10 minutes. This takes out any 'yellowness'.*
- *Forget expensive spot creams: a dab of toothpaste on the spot overnight could do the trick.*
- *For a cellulite-busting body scrub, don't throw away your coffee grinds! Drain off the coffee and mix a handful with your regular shower gel, rubbing liberally over your dimply bits. Coffee contains plenty of caffeine, which is an ingredient in lots of fancy anti-cellulite creams. It's also got oil in it so your skin is nice and smooth afterwards.*
- *Eke out nail polish by adding a couple of drops of remover to the bottle and giving it a good shake.*

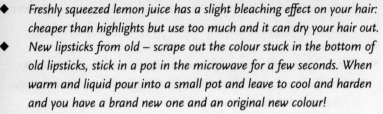

◆ *Freshly squeezed lemon juice has a slight bleaching effect on your hair:*
  cheaper than highlights but use too much and it can dry your hair out.

◆ *New lipsticks from old – scrape out the colour stuck in the bottom of*
  old lipsticks, stick in a pot in the microwave for a few seconds. When
  warm and liquid pour into a small pot and leave to cool and harden
  and you have a brand new one and an original new colour!

◆ *Save any small sample bottles and refill from your regular shampoo*
  or moisturiser before you go on holiday. Saves a fortune on buying
  the special travel bottles at over £1 a go from M&S or Superdrug.

◆ *According to the Old-Style boards, the model Marie Helvin swore by*
  slathering her face in mayonnaise and rinsing off. Old-Stylers have
  tested and reckon it's good!

◆ *Place cold tea bags or cucumber slices over your eyes as a quick pick-*
  me-up.

◆ *If it's good enough for Cleopatra... add milk to your bathwater, just a*
  cup is fine and feels fabulous. Or cheap dried milk powder is reckoned
  to work nearly as well.

◆ *Make your own 'Sugar Scrub' – half a cup of brown sugar, one-*
  eighth of a cup of vegetable oil, 1 tablespoon of honey and some
  essential oils like rosemary, mint or grapefruit. Use about
  1 tablespoon, especially on rough dishpan hands, elbows and feet.

◆ *Adding a handful of oatmeal to your bath will soften the skin.*

◆ *Use the skin of an avocado to soften elbows.*

◆ *Rinse fine hair in beer to give it more body.*

◆ *An egg yolk on hair is a great conditioner and makes it shiny, but*
  rinse off in cold water or you'll have scrambled egg in your hair!

◆ *Shaving cream massaged into your scalp and then removed with cold*

water helps clear dandruff without buying expensive dandruff-busting
shampoos.

◆   Use cold milk as an eye makeup remover and cleanser.

◆   To make your perfume go further apply a thin layer of petroleum jelly,
    like Vaseline, to your skin and spray on perfume. It will 'stick' to the
    oily area and last longer.

◆   Forget expensive 'hot oil' conditioning treatments for your hair. Olive
    oil massaged in will work just as well but rinse thoroughly.

◆   For tired eyes and dark circles, mash up some banana and put under
    your eyes for 10 minutes. The potassium helps the dark circles.

◆   An expensive body lotion can be 'stretched' by mixing with cheaper,
    unscented body lotion.

◆   Sugar or salt mixed with baby oil rubbed on your face and then
    washed off does the job as well as some expensive exfoliators.

Home-made Yummy Face Masks

Strawberry and Oat Exfoliating Mask
2 tbsp ground oats
3 large ripe strawberries
1 tsp single cream

Grind oats to a fine powder using a pestle and mortar. Mash up
strawberries and mix with the oats. Add enough cream to make a
paste. Apply the pack to your face and leave on for 10 minutes. Gently
remove with cool water then pat dry.

Honey Face Mask

Massage a small amount of heated honey over your face and leave on for 15 minutes. You can add wheat germ which acts as an abrasive and exfoliates the dead skin.

Apricot Face Mask

Great for dry skin. Mix fresh or dried mashed apricots with warm olive oil to form a spreadable paste. Apply, leave on for 10 minutes and rinse off.

Sunburn Treatments

Okay, so we all know prevention is better than cure with this one but in the unlikely event it happens to you (and obviously if it's serious the local hospital is your first port of call)...

- *Dab cool tea on burnt areas.*
- *Use any 'aloe vera' moisturiser, as it's one of the major cooling ingredients in branded after-sun products.*
- *Try supermarket own brands of after-sun instead of the posh makes like Ambre Solaire which can be expensive.*
- *Put natural live yoghurt on your burnt bits, leave it on till it 'sets' then wash off with cool water.*
- *Use slices of cucumber.*

More Thrifty Beauty Tips

◆ *Most make-up counters offer 'free' makeovers. Some might push you a bit to buy the products but a polite 'No thank you' should be okay. Body Shop and Boots are among those that do. Even at the more expensive counters that charge you an upfront fee, you can often redeem your booking fee against purchases, so wait till you need something and book a makeover at the same time. Some MoneySaving brides have used this as the wedding make-up makeover!*

◆ *Don't be afraid to ask for free samples. They'll often decant foundation or moisturiser into little bottles for you to try; great for taking on holiday and means you've got a decent amount to try rather than in those fiddly sachets you get free in magazines.*

◆ *Local beauty colleges often offer huge discounts on salon prices for massages and facials. Old-Stylers reckon on paying around £5 for a facial compared with £30 upwards at salons, so pop down there and ask or keep a lookout for ads in the local paper.*

◆ *It's the same story with hairdressing – most hairdressing colleges hold discount nights. Students are supervised so you won't come out with green hair having gone in for a trim, or if you live in any of the big cities try the Toni & Guy Training Academy.*

Don't Forget the Freebies

And don't forget to pull out all those 'free' sachets of shampoo, moisturiser and the like that come with magazines. If you're staying in hotels make sure you take the shampoo, soap and all the bathroom toiletries; after all, you've paid to use the room so if you don't use them in the hotel you can use them at home. Taking towels and dressing gowns isn't MoneySaving, however – it's theft!

Chapter 3

CLOTHES AND SHOES

There's no getting away from it – clothes are one of life's essentials. We all need them (unless you're a budding naturist!) but how much do we spend on them? Surveys tell us that women spend nearly £100,000 on clothes in a lifetime (£96,720 to be precise), over an estimated 65 years of shopping!

And, let's be honest, how much of the stuff you buy do you actually wear? In reality, we wear something like 20 per cent of our wardrobe 80 per cent of the time, so the vast majority of it just hangs there gathering dust, or worse still, hidden in its original carrier bag complete with price tag!

It's time to revise your shopping habits and think 'vintage', not 'charity', and 'Primark', not 'Prada'!

CHARITY STARTS AT HOME...

Well, as near as your local charity shop anyway. Charity shops can be an absolute goldmine and can save you a fortune when you only need something once, say a new suit for a job interview, a spare scarf or practical basics like school uniform for the kids. Many people chuck out the contents of their wardrobe simply because they're bored with their clothes, and not because they're falling to bits, so there are some serious bargains to be had.

Think 'Posh'

◆ *Head for charity shops in the posh part of town as they tend to have better-quality stuff, and you might pick up some designer labels on the cheap. Some of the celebs living around London's exclusive Primrose Hill and Hampstead areas have been seen dropping off black bags at their local charity shops so it's worth having a look if you're in London for the day. Likewise, in some of the posher parts of Manchester and Cheshire where the footballers' wives set hang out you might come across some really good designer gear.*

◆ *It's worth checking out the smaller independent charity shops too, as the larger chains, like Oxfam, tend to be more expensive and often recognise anything with a designer label and may charge more for it.*

Charity Shop the Savvy Way

◆ *Before embarking on any shopping expedition take the time to go through your existing wardrobe and work out what you really, really need. Have you got 10 pairs of black trousers and jeans but hardly any tops or shirts? Or maybe you've got loads of cheap and cheerful summer clothes but no winter jumpers. Make a list and keep it in your handbag or wallet so it's always with you when you bargain hunt.*

◆ *Jot down all the family's measurements in a notebook and never go out without it. And keep a tape measure with you. (Don't be afraid to ask to borrow one if you've forgotten yours!)*

◆ *Stick to all the usual shopping rules; so even if it's cheap don't buy it unless you need it, it fits, you like it and you'll actually wear it. Stuff you'll 'diet into' is always a waste of money and never buy unless you're 100 per cent sure; there are always more bargains out there.*

◆ *Curtains are often a good buy in charity shops or even on eBay so have a list of your window measurements with you. They're often in good nick as most people get rid of them simply because they've changed their colour scheme or moved house. Children's curtains, particularly character ones, can be good value as most children only go through phases of wanting Winnie the Pooh, Action Man or Barbie so they're unlikely to have had much wear.*

◆ *Charity shops are great for fun 'one-off' items and stuff for fancy-dress parties or the kids' dressing-up box, but look out for the 'classics' too. These won't date, and people out there with more money than sense tend to get rid of their perfectly good clothes very quickly with little wear.*

◆ *Go for clothes you can adapt. Okay, so you may hate its buttons but if you can pick up a shirt for £2 and change the buttons it's worth it. Plain skirts can be unpicked and if you're handy with a sewing machine you can reuse the material or turn trousers into shorts.*

◆ *Jumpers are a great bargain; even if you don't like the style, buy for the wool. Unpick and learn to knit or bribe a relative to knit you your own individual 'one-off' jumper.*

◆ *How many times have you spilt paint down a still-decent pair of jeans while decorating or got an oil stain on your jumper fixing the car? Stock up on your decorating and DIY clothes on the cheap. Buy cheap, comfy trousers and T-shirts because it won't matter when you've got paint all down you and you can throw them away when you've finished or save till next time.*

◆ *Set aside plenty of time for clothes shopping. Never ever do it in a rush – that's when you end up impulse buying or buying something horrendous. This is a waste, even at charity shop prices.*

◆ *Customise items you buy from charity shops, jumble or car boot sales with your own beads, buttons and trimmings.*

◆ *Network! Pop in regularly to your local charity shops and get to know the staff. Chances are they'll drop their prices for you and you might get first rummage out the back when they have new stock in!*

KEEP IT IN THE FAMILY

Beg, borrow and steal (well, not quite) from your relatives. Granny's wardrobe can be a little goldmine – think 'vintage', not 'old-fashioned'.

Let's face it – if you're an avid follower of fashion those trends will come round again.

REAL OLD-STYLE STORY

When my Gran died I raided her wardrobe as my aunts were going to donate her stuff to the charity shop. I ended up with several pairs of gorgeous leather gloves, some lovely tea dresses from the 1940s as well as some pretty slips and petticoats. I also got loads of costume jewellery which my Gran had stopped wearing because some of it had been out of date, but now it's back in fashion and people have been positively drooling over the brooches! I just wish my mum had kept all her clothes from the 50s and 60s – oooh, I hate her for throwing them away!

CUSTOMISE, DON'T CHUCK!

◆ *Bored with it but can't justify getting rid of it? Customise your clothes to give them a new look. Think 'Sienna Miller' style and check out eBay, boot sales, charity shops and jumble sales for great second-hand bargains. Most people de-cluttering their wardrobe will be glad to get something for their stuff.*

◆ *And once you've tired of your customised clothes sell them on eBay or at boot fairs to get some money back.*

◆ *Dye clothes or shoes. Wedding day shoes that have been worn only once can be dyed black for loads more wear.*

◆ *'Shop' from your own wardrobe. Wear some of those things you keep for 'best' and try out new combinations and things you've never worn or left in suitcases in the loft. Wearing some of your 'best' things makes you feel good, brightens up the day and saves money!*

REAL OLD-STYLE STORY

Find a really good, old-fashioned cobbler. This might sound a bit extravagant but a good cobbler can rescue and restore even the most badly-treated shoes for much less than it would cost to buy a new pair.

Learn to Sew

◆ *Make the most of free patterns in magazines. The ones in Prima are really rated by the Old-Style community, and if they're not for you then swap them.*

◆ *Or make your own. Draw round an old top or skirt on a piece of newspaper, leaving a one-inch gap all the way round. Use this as your pattern, but bear in mind this method tends to work better with simple designs. Local haberdashery shops often sell offcuts and remnants of material, trimmings and the like, and even John Lewis has a bargain box. So much cheaper than buying material off the roll.*

◆ *Can't get your hands on any free patterns? Try www.sewingpatterns.com and download your own.*

◆ *Yep, all very well this sewing lark but what happens if you haven't got a sewing machine? Check out car boot sales or the small ads – you can pick up second-hand machines for around £10 or try www.freecycle.org where people post up items they don't want and are happy to give to a good home.*

◆ *If you want to buy new you can pick up a basic model at Argos for around £80 or try your local sewing shop where Old-Stylers have picked up second-hand 'trade in' models for around £25.*

◆ *Running up school uniform on a machine, particularly summer dresses for girls, can be a real MoneySaver; you can pick up the gingham checked material that's used for around £3.*

REAL OLD-STYLE STORY

I took a basic pattern-cutting course last year. You'd be surprised how easy it is to make a skirt pattern that's a perfect fit. A couple of months ago, I saw a great skirt online, but at £80, it was not to be. So I did my own version. It took maybe 30 minutes, plus another couple of hours to sew it. All in all, the skirt cost around £6, and it looks almost as good as the £80 one.

Make the Most of What You've Got!

No excuse now for not giving your clothes a new lease of life!

◆ *Turn your tatty or ripped jeans into shorts or make them into bags or draught-excluders by cutting off the legs, stuffing them and stitching up the ends.*

◆ *Cut down T-shirts for crop tops.*

◆ *Baby socks make great scratch mitts; they fit better and the elastic helps them stay on better.*

◆ *Save first- and second-year baby trousers and turn them into shorts for the next year with pinking shears and a bit of wonder web. It only works for two years because of the nappy capacity which allows for growth room!*

Sock Stuff

Loads of uses for old, shrunken, mismatched socks:

◆ *Turn them into dusters, shoe polishers and car cleaning rags.*

◆ *Stick them over the end of the tops of step ladders when you're leaning them against an inside wall to save marking the wallpaper.*

◆ *Sew them up with pot pourri inside and stick them inside your shoes to keep them sweet-smelling.*

◆ *Use them as shoe covers when packing your suitcase.*

◆ *Give them to your local school or playgroup for puppet making.*

◆ *They make instant, cheap toys for your dog. Stuff them and tie up the ends.*

- Great for using to keep your toes warm if you're unlucky enough to end up with your leg in plaster – those casts where your toes stick out the end getting draughty! One Old-Styler claims she got through her entire supply of old socks when her three-year-old broke his leg a few years back!
- Hang on to them for an extra thermal layer in the winter.
- Stick a couple of pairs over your hands when your cat or dog comes in from the wet, stroke them with the socks on to dry them off. This saves using household towels and they love the fuss!
- Good for storing onions.

And Don't Forget those Old Tights . . .
- Hang them in the garage to store flower bulbs or onions.
- Use them as plant ties.
- Ask your local school, cub group or whatever if they would like them for making 'cress-heads'. Or make your own with the kids. Get the leg of a pair of tights, pour cress seeds in the toe, put in a layer of kitchen paper, stuff with more tights until you have a grapefruit-sized ball then tie a knot. Dampen, turn it upside down and watch the cress sprout from the top. Stick it in a mug or something and you can draw faces on with magic markers.
- Pack loads together inside one leg and use as a mild abrasive cleaner for your sink, shower or bath.
- Use for stuffing inside home-made soft toys, or to plump out 'squashed' pillows and cushions.
- Make a soap holder to attach to the garden tap.
- Wrap around ordinary coat hangers to turn them into padded ones for your best clothes.

◆ *They make great 'fly squashers' when washing the car. They're gentle enough not to scratch the paintwork but will lift off the flies easily! Scrunch them up, soak in soapy water and rub gently.*

And the Rest of Your Undies?

◆ *Underpants make great floor cloths; old T-shirts make nightshirts; the list is endless . . .*

◆ *Save old clothes for packing when you move rather than buying packaging. Knickers are great for plates as the extra padding keeps them from chipping. Socks are great for glasses or breakables, and pillows make good packing for computers.*

◆ *Worn-out clothes but love the fabric? Cut them up for patchwork or use, say, the velvet from a skirt to turn into a posh scarf. You can also use the material to cover notebooks, picture frames or make rag rugs. Make coverings for dolls' house furniture, including mini 'towels' and 'rugs' and dolls' clothes.*

'Black Bag Parties'

Can't be bothered with getting up at the crack of dawn for boot fairs, not mastered the art of eBay? Have a clothes-swapping party!

REAL OLD-STYLE STORY

A couple of years ago my friend started what we now call 'Black Bag Night'. The idea's simple. You set aside a night for a group of people to meet at someone's house. Everybody collects their unwanted clothes and shoes, cleans them if necessary, piles them into a bag and brings them along.

The items are put into a big pile and one by one the hostess (or host!) holds up an item to see if there are any takers. If there's more than one person interested, the item goes into the fight pile to be argued over later on! At the end of the night any leftover items are put aside to be taken to the charity shop (or sold on eBay if you're really keen!)

The only rule is that there are no judgements made – we've all bought things we wish we hadn't! Putting the items into a big pile at the start of the night helps as it makes those fashion *faux pas* a little more anonymous!

It's a fantastic way of having a fun cheap night out (they're always more fun if you bring along some nibbles and wine) and you get some new clothes into the bargain. It always amazes me that people want things that I just can't stand any more! The wider the circle of people, the more variety you'll get.

And don't just stop at clothes! We've found books, CDs and DVDs pretty popular, and now we pretty much bring along any unwanted odds and ends – handbags, jewellery, fairy lights, we've had them all.

Clothes swaps are a brilliant idea; you can get a whole new summer or winter wardrobe at a fraction of the high-street cost, and it's a chance to get your hands on your friend's jacket, dress or jeans that you've always liked.

Maximise Your Wardrobe

◆　*Wait for a rainy Sunday afternoon and spend a bit of time sorting through your clothes. Sort them into colour groups and then look at which colours match and complement each other. Then see what you've got in each pile that you could wear with something from a matching/complementary colour pile. This really opens your eyes to new combinations of stuff you'd never thought about wearing together before. You should end up with a whole set of 'new' outfits without spending money. And if you've got an old Polaroid camera sitting around you can take snaps of the 'new' combinations and stick them to the wardrobe door for those 'I haven't got a thing to wear' days.*

◆　*Hang on to magazine pictures of outfits you like; chances are you can re-create the look from items already in your wardrobe.*

◆　*Check out supermarket ranges, particularly the Tesco 'value' range, where you can pick up plain white T-shirts and long-sleeved tops for just a couple of pounds, and even nab a pair of jeans for around £4.*

HIGH STREET SHOPS

Primark is the store that even those at the cutting-edge of fashion are talking about. It's worth checking out for budget-priced versions of many designer and expensive high-street styles – you can pick up a coat for around £10. Matalan and Tesco's 'Florence + Fred' range are worth a look. Tesco's budget-priced version of the green 'Chloé' dress Kylie wore a couple of years back later appeared at more than double the price on eBay with people desperate to get their hands on it. And think TK Maxx, Uniqlo, Peacocks, Asda and New Look for budget-priced clothes and accessories. Most have a range for men, women and children.

LOOK AFTER YOUR CLOTHES

◆   *Store out-of-season clothes in a vac-bag or large suitcase, in the loft or under a bed. This leaves more room in your wardrobe and drawers for stuff you use and saves it all getting scrunched up and ruined. You can see what you've got and what you might need to replace more easily.*

◆   *Put scrunched-up balls of newspaper in unworn shoes and store them in their boxes to keep them dust-free. Polish them regularly and have them re-heeled so they'll last longer.*

◆   *Wrap tissue paper round any delicate clothes or those with beading on them. No need to buy new – save tissue paper from old shoe boxes or packaging.*

◆   *Don't worry too much about what you wear when you're going to be home alone all day; you can get away with old clothes. Okay, Trinny and Susannah may not be impressed but they're not likely to pop in, are they?*

◆ *And don't fall into the trap of sticking everything in the washing machine after just one wear. Okay, so you're not going to wear a T-shirt with curry stains down the front (are you?) or a shirt stinking of stale BO, but if it's just a small mark, sponge it off and then wear it for a second day 'round the house'. Or stick it on a hanger for an airing. Washing and tumble drying your clothes less will prolong their life.*

CHILDREN'S CLOTHES

If you've got friends with children who are a bit older than your own, ask them to tell you if they're getting rid of any clothes. Some people feel embarrassed to offer 'castoffs' to others but one person's trash is another's treasure and all that. Set up a regular clothes-swap or 'black bag' circle among friends or parents from school for either your own or your kids' stuff. And if you've no friends with kids of a similar age, make friends with the neighbours! Don't be too proud to take clothes – small kids tend to wreck stuff anyway so why pay a fortune when it may only last a few months? Even if it's just jumpers or jeans that the kids can play out in or use for walks in the park, it's worth it and saves mucking up new stuff.

Knitting Patterns for Babies

There are lots of sites for downloading knitting patterns – a few to try that are recommended on the Old-Style boards are: www.bevscountrycottage.com, www.knitting.about.com and www.chicknits.com

There's a whole thread on Old-Style about crochet: check it out at www.moneysavingexpert.com/oscrochet

Buying and Selling Children's Clothes

◆   *Look out for local table-top sales, sales run by the National Childbirth Trust or car boot fairs.*

◆   *Ask friends if they know of any local quality second-hand shops that sell on baby equipment and clothes. If you're selling there's usually no fee to pay but once sold the shop will take a percentage of the profit.*

◆   *When selling at a car boot fair, make sure items are clean, safe and not overpriced. Don't get too greedy and you can clear the lot and go home with an empty car!*

◆   *The 50p bin in charity shops is a goldmine for baby clothes. Old-Stylers have spotted brand-new and designer gear in here, which having been bought up and worn they've sold on for profit on eBay!*

SELL, SELL, SELL!

Okay, we've done the buying and swapping bit but eventually you'll need to get shot of it one way or another.

Check out your local phone book for second-hand clothes shops that will sell on decent-quality stuff, suits, dresses and labelled pieces. These will need to be in good condition so if it's a bit tatty it might be best left for the boot fair. The way it works in most of these shops is that you get a cut of whatever the item sells for, but it's aimed at your quality stuff, not cheap and cheerful basics.

eBay and boot fairs are also worth a go and you'll pretty much get the full selling price, bar a small fee on eBay and the price of your pitch at the boot fair.

eBay

eBay ranks pretty high on the list for selling but it seems that getting the right bids can be the luck of the draw. Some Old-Stylers have managed to shift their stuff on the auction site while others haven't taken any bids. One solution for hard-to-shift stuff is to bundle it up and sell in bulk rather than as individual items.

◆ *Keep items to one size and either one store or a high street mix – M&S, Zara and so on – whereas designer labels are more likely to go on their own.*

◆ *Or group them all as, say, size 12 suits or size 10 exercise clothes and so on.*

◆ *Always, always have a picture of the clothes and start the bidding low. More successful Old-Stylers reckon starting between 50p and £1 is a good bet.*

◆ *It's also been suggested that you talk up your worldly goods, using phrases like 'exquisite', 'unique', 'vintage' or 'rare' in the hope of selling them, but make sure you're not telling fibs! Be accurate with your descriptions, sizes and any marks or signs of wear.*

Flogging clothes can often be a seasonal thing. Come the New Year or summer, you're competing with the high street sales, so it's worth waiting at that point.

When to Buy and Sell

Evening wear bargains (ball gowns, cocktail dresses and the like) are best snapped up in January as the shops always over-stock evening wear before Christmas. Some of the dresses can double up as bridesmaids' dresses even though they're not labelled this way (and of course they're cheaper than going to a posh wedding shop!) Try dress hire shops too; some sell off last season's dresses twice a year and many discount heavily depending on how many times the item has been worn. Bearing in mind a lot of these items will be designer, costing hundreds of pounds, you can pick them up for a fraction of the price.

BEG AND BORROW

Forget spending a fortune on a 'one-off' outfit for a wedding, night out, interview or funeral. Always 'borrow' outfits if you can – most people will happily lend hats or suits for weddings and you can mix and match along with your own accessories or borrow some from other friends.

Wedding Dresses

The ultimate 'wear it once' item, though some Old-Stylers claim to have worn their wedding dresses a second time round and even a third or fourth! Rather than buy – and depending on where you shop they can cost a small fortune – look at hiring, making, borrowing or revamping one that's been in the family for years. But if you've splashed out on the big white meringue number here's what to do once the big day has come and gone.

◆ *Make it into your first child's christening dress.*

◆ *Sell on eBay or through small ads for money to spend on something else.*

◆ *Keep for your future daughter, niece or family friend to wear.*

◆ *Wear it to your divorce party! (Yes, this really was a tried-and-tested suggestion on the Old-Style boards!)*

◆ *Have the skirt part shortened and wear it as a cocktail dress.*

◆ *Dye it to wear as an evening gown.*

◆ *Save for your children for dressing up 'Princess' style.*

◆ *Make into a pair of curtains.*

◆ *Use the silk part to make scatter cushions.*

◆ *Make the train into a ballet dress.*

Chapter 4

HOME MAINTENANCE AND DIY

It isn't unusual to spend £7,000 a year on DIY projects round the house; that's everything from fixing dripping taps to full-scale loft conversions, double glazing and conservatories. Add that up over an average 50 years of home ownership and you'll have shelled out around £300,000, more than the average house price.

And there's no shortage of 'expert' tradespeople out there willing to take your money to bodge the job for you. So if you decide to go it alone, how can you cut your costs without risking the roof falling down round your ears?

With the huge rise in television makeover shows, most people aren't content with slapping on a coat of paint; they want 'the look'. So this chapter's all about how to accessorise your house on a budget.

When it finally comes to selling up there's suggestions for the best way to spruce up your house and get the place sold.

DIY, PLUMBING AND HOME MAINTENANCE

Before you tackle any DIY jobs round the house or garden, make sure it's something you feel comfortable doing. Over 200,000 accidents occur at home every year as a result of rushed, bodged or over-enthusiastic DIY, so while you might think you can save some cash doing the job yourself, it's a false economy if you're going to spend a few thousand calling in the professionals to put it right, not to mention ending up in A&E!

And while most people can manage to slap on a coat of paint, never attempt a spot of DIY on the electrics unless you're a qualified electrician. Since January 2005, new legislation has tightened the rules on what you can and can't do with your household electrics. You can still do simple jobs like replacing light switch covers or changing a ceiling rose, providing it's part of an existing circuit, but if you need to put in a new circuit or, say, put a light in your garden shed you'll need to have the job done professionally by a qualified electrician, or get approval from your local building control office if you do the work yourself. Attempting DIY electrics without approval or the right qualifications can mean a huge fine and problems selling your house if you don't have the correct paperwork.

For more information or to find a government-approved electrician, contact an organisation like www.niceic.org.uk (National Inspection Council for Electrical Installation Contracting).

If you're using power tools, always use a plug-in 'RCD' (residual current device). They'll 'trip' the current should you cut through a cable. They cost around £10 in DIY stores.

DIY Jobs

◆ Carry out household repairs as soon as you notice something's wrong. The old 'prevention is better than cure' adage still holds true. Leaving a dripping tap for a few weeks or months in the hope it will cure itself is just asking for trouble; the problem's likely to get much worse, and what starts off as a five-minute job changing a washer ends up as a huge plumber's bill.

◆ Think 'make do and mend'. Keep a box to hand with all your old screws, nails, nuts and bolts, spare bulbs and fuses. One Old-Styler lost two screws from his Yale lock just before Christmas which meant the entire locking mechanism fell off. A brand-new lock would have cost around £20 but thanks to a couple of trusty screws from his 'odd job box' the job was done in double-quick time for free!

◆ Keep another box with spare bits of wire, offcuts of wood, bulldog clips, masking tape, even spare glue from old flatpack kits – you never know when they'll come in handy!

◆ Borrow power tools from friends or neighbours. Hiring and buying can be expensive and often it's only needed just the once so get to work on that community spirit. Do remember to give them back though!

◆ For free advice, speak to builders' merchants and trade electrical or plumbing outlets. Be friendly and they'll probably give you a few tips and tell you how to do it yourself.

◆ If you're unsure about any job it's worth getting at least three quotes for the work before you start wielding your sledgehammer! Just think of all those 'Houses from Hell'-type programmes where amateur DIY has gone wrong.

How to . . . Kitchens and Bathrooms

◆ *Get the rubber seal back on a washing machine*
Taken it off to clean and can't get it back on? Try putting a good
squirt of washing-up liquid on the rubber and give it a good stretch
before trying to fit it back on. Or soak it in hot water to make it
springy again.

◆ *Unblock the hole at the bottom of the fridge where the liquid
drains away*
Pour an eggcup of white vinegar down the hole, then add about a
teaspoon of bicarb (or as much of it as you can get down there), wait
for it to fizz and then screw up a sheet of kitchen roll into a sausage
shape and stick the pointed end down the hole to soak up the excess
liquid. If the hole's big enough, get a straw down there and blow
really hard to shift all the debris.

◆ *Clean up filthy grouting in bathrooms and kitchens*
Most of those brand-name 'mould and mildew' cleaners are nothing
more than diluted bleach packaged up in a fancy spray gun. It's
much cheaper to make your own. Use undiluted bleach scrubbed on
the grouting with an old toothbrush or use whitening cleaner, the sort
of stuff that's sold to be used on kids' plimsolls.

◆ *Get transfers off bathroom tiles*
Yep, those lovely stick-on transfers have now taken root on the tiles and it's decorating time – how to get them off? Razor blades can be used to scrape off the excess and then any glue remains washed off with hot soapy water. It's also worth using nail varnish remover, but test a small inconspicuous area first.

◆ *Get rid of condensation*
A quick way is to open the windows to allow the air to circulate. A bowl of salt in the room helps too. It's basically the lack of air circulation that causes condensation when warm air hits the cold window and then releases water vapour into the air. To help with the condensation problem in the bathroom, try running cold water into the bath before the hot water. A dehumidifier is another option but obviously costs a bit more. Also, try cutting a potato in half, rubbing on the window and buffing up with a dry cloth.

◆ *Descale a shower head*
Unscrew it and leave in a sink full of vinegar and hot water for at least an hour. If there's lots of limescale it may need doing again; if so, give it a good scrub in between.

◆ *Fix a noisy toilet*
Install a Torbec or Fluidmaster silent fill valve – these valves are a universal fit and will replace the existing ball valve.

◆ **Fix wobbly bathroom taps**
You need to buy two plastic top hat connectors. These are small plastic connectors that fit under the basin and locate between the tap and the nut which secures the tap to the basin. They cost 30p each and, yes, you will need a tap spanner which is designed for the job.

◆ **Fix a stiff cold water tap**
Isolate the cold water supply, remove the body of the tap, replace the washer and clean up with lubricating solution. WD40 should do.

◆ **Stop a dripping tap**
You need to change the washer. Isolate the water supply, remove the body of the tap with a spanner and fit a new washer.

How to . . . Decorating

◆ **Get rid of glue on walls**
Stripped off the wallpaper but now left with residual glue on the walls? Wash down with sugar soap (which you can buy at your local hardware shop) and elbow grease.

◆ **Replaster walls**
Instead of replastering pock-marked walls, simply mix a paste of Polyfilla and very thinly smear it on the wall with a scraper (the wider the better). Then after it's dry simply get a damp cloth and wipe over and you'll have nice smooth walls.

Fix a peeling ceiling
Give it a rough sand (don't forget your mask), then apply PVA glue and let it dry for 24 hours before painting. If for some reason some bits are still sticking out then scrape them and reapply glue. Apply a few thick coats of paint to give a smooth finish.

 Get a smooth finish on walls
For newly plastered walls, mix one-third PVA glue and two-thirds water and brush on. Let it dry before painting.

 Clean painted walls
Sugar soap is the best bet. Use it with warm water and one of those squidgy cloths to wash down the walls. Or try warm water with a little washing-up liquid. Depending on the paint used in the first place, some marks wipe off easier than others. Highly recommended when you're slapping a coat up is Dulux Real Life Matt emulsion for easy cleaning.

 Make a cheap filler
To repair old ceilings, paste newspaper over the loose parts; this sets hard like papier-mâché. Can also be used scrunched up to fill holes in doors.

 Relay a carpet
Got to move the carpet to work on the floor beneath? What's the easiest way to relay the carpet without calling in the professionals? If it's hessian-backed, unhook it carefully from the gripper and roll up –

don't fold it. You shouldn't need to stretch it before laying back. If it's felt-backed, go round the edges with a spray glue to fix it back down. For rubber-backed carpets, be careful when you're pulling them up as the rubber can stick to the floor.

◆ **Fix creaky stairs**
For a cheap and cheerful fix, try talcum powder between the boards.

How To . . . Miscellaneous

◆ **Make coat hooks**
Save offcuts of wood from making shelves, for example. These small bits of plank can be painted (with leftover paint or sample pots) and then you can fix coat hooks or small knobs along, drill a hole at either end and you have a hook rail for coats or for children's rooms. Or you can glue wooden clothes pegs along for a paperwork holder for kitchen or office.

◆ **Fix jammed locks**
A quick squirt of WD40 should do the trick.

◆ **Get rid of scratches on a fish tank**
Duraglit brass polishing wool will get rid of most scratches or try a smokers' toothpaste like Clinomyn.

◆ **Stop a door squeaking**
*Rub a candle stub around the area where the hinges meet. In
extreme cases the door may need to be taken off and the candle
rubbed on the inside pin of the hinges. This technique is also good for
drawers that won't slide easily. Rub a candle stub on the runners or
the bits of wood that touch the unit itself.*

◆ **Take the gouges out of laminate flooring**
*If something heavy has been dropped and the floor's compressed get
a damp tea towel and iron over the dent. Or you can buy 'filler'
crayons, like kids' wax crayons in different colours, or raid the kids'
bedroom for a matching felt-tip pen to use to colour over the scratch.*

DECORATING

Give your home the *Changing Rooms* touch if you don't want Laurence
Llewellyn Bowen traipsing through it or Colin and Justin tearing down
your newly decorated bedroom.

◆ *For great rugs, ask a local carpet store for old samples (end of season
when they're updating their ranges is good). They can be patched
together with gaffer tape underneath.*
◆ *Check out charity shops for curtains, bedding, pictures and frames.*
◆ *Second-hand furniture can look great with a new coat of paint or
some new handles from the DIY store.*
◆ *A quick makeover for cheap furniture is to sand or strip it and paint it*

in light matt or silk colours which you then 'distress' by lightly sanding it once the paint is dry.

◆ Horrible cheap woodchip laminate furniture can be revamped by sticking on false panelling. Repaint using laminate paint and add some old-fashioned knobs and handles.

◆ Coffee table tops that are too scratched to repair can be re-covered using 'Fablon', which you can get from DIY stores or craft shops. They do a really realistic rosewood at about £4 a metre.

◆ Cover up stained or frayed furniture with Indian-style throws you can buy cheaply from 'ethnic' shops.

◆ For inexpensive prints on the walls buy cheap frames from pound shops and put old prints/postcards in them or even use unusual wallpaper designs. Or you can buy cheap second-hand books with coloured pictures in them, cut these out and frame them.

◆ It's not always necessary to replace dodgy-coloured tiles. They can be repainted with special tile paint bought from places like B&Q and Homebase.

◆ Mix up new paint colours from whatever colours are left in the shed. Most people have a tin of white somewhere which can be used to dilute down a strong colour.

◆ For painting small areas, buy a couple of little 'match pots' — much cheaper than a whole tin of paint that won't be used.

◆ An inexpensive way to give a kitchen a new lease of life is to change the colour of one wall and choose accessories to match. Pick these up at boot fairs, second-hand shops or markets.

Painting and Decorating

◆ *Painting is generally more cost-effective than papering as wallpaper shows signs of wear on the corners, whereas painted walls can just be washed down to remove marks and sticky fingerprints.*

◆ *To paint skirting boards without giving the carpet a coat of paint, roll it back or stick masking tape along the carpet edge while painting. Or try tucking some newspaper under the skirting board to avoid painting on wooden floors.*

◆ *Supermarkets now do their own range of home furnishings; cushions, bed covers and the like. Check these out before heading for department stores that can be more pricey, or mix and match the two.*

◆ *For discounts on curtains and upholstery fabric, go to places like Fabric World (www.fabricworldlondon.co.uk).*

◆ *Matching up existing wallpaper can be difficult if it's a few years since buying the original rolls. Rather than tearing the lot down and starting again, it's always worth taking a picture of the pattern and sending it to the manufacturer to see if they have any spare rolls or excess lying around.*

◆ *A gallon of paint will give any room a complete facelift. Always check out the 'oops' gallons at DIY stores; people request colours and never pick them up, or the person mixing the paint doesn't get the shade quite right. Sometimes the colours can be a tad putrid, but occasionally you'll find a gorgeous colour that's a steal!*

REAL OLD-STYLE STORY

The other day some workmen came to clear out the house next-door-but-one. They were about to throw a 6-litre tin of Dulux paint in the back of the van when I caught them and asked if I could have it.

Finishing Touches

◆ *Try Matalan, Woolworths and the supermarket 'home' ranges for budget-priced home furnishings like quilts, cushions, kitchen equipment, candles and vases.*

◆ *Keep any beautiful glass jars, bottles and other pretty containers you get. Scrub off any labels and decant cheap bath products into them. Makes bathrooms look very posh. Can also be used to keep odds and ends in.*

◆ *Don't buy those expensive 'coffee table'-style interior design books new – borrow from the library or pick up at a car boot sale.*

◆ *Re-cover seat pads on chairs to match curtains or give them a new lease of life. You just need a large staple gun and some fabric which you can pick up in the remnant box at your local haberdashery store or charity shop. The hardest part is getting the tension right all the way around but it's better than buying a new set of chairs every time you change your colour scheme.*

- When doing up a nursery or child's bedroom, buy two sets of curtains. Hang one pair and make new seat pads, cushions, a pillowcase and even a cot-size duvet cover for older babies with the other.
- Factory or clearance shops are worth a visit; for example, Denby pottery has 12 shops throughout the UK selling seconds at up to 20 per cent off (www.denby.co.uk).
- As an alternative to those expensive kitchen utensil storage jars you can buy in places like John Lewis, use an old bread bin or lunch box, or even paint some old plant pots to hold your scourers, cloths and brushes.
- If you ever have Chinese takeaways, save those lovely plastic containers, wash them up and they make great boxes for sewing stuff, pencils for the kids and fit neatly in the computer desk.

REAL OLD-STYLE STORY

Browsing through those expensive interior design books, one idea particularly caught my eye – beautiful, mismatched but elegant china pots in the bathroom cabinet for all of those bits and bobs that usually live in scruffy plastic bags. The photos looked fantastic but the sources – new and antique shops – were definitely aimed at the Notting Hill set. I turned out some of my cupboards and found all sorts of beautiful little pots and bowls that I don't use and had been planning to send to the charity shop. A plain white

> ceramic sugar bowl I found looked identical to the £40 bowl
> in the photos. An old glass jar I'd kept for years because I
> liked the shape is now an elegant receptacle for all my emery
> boards. The inside of the cupboard looks terribly chic, just
> like the books and magazines, and I haven't spent a penny.
> What a result.

GENERAL STUFF

Manuals and Instruction Books

Found an old computer in the loft but without the instructions, or
been given a television but not sure how to retune it? Check out
www.instruction-manuals.co.uk, a website that gets heaps of praise on
the Old-Style boards. It lists loads of electrical and household
products. Once you've found your make and model, click on it and
then it either redirects you to the manufacturer's own website to
download a free copy of the instructions or tells you the current
situation of the company, if it's been taken over, gone bust or
whatever.

It's also worth trying the manufacturer – either do a Google
search and find their website to see if there are any free downloads or
ring them and ask if they can stick a copy in the post. Be nice to them
as it might save you getting charged.

For spare parts try www.spares2go.co.uk – it's a home counties-
based company that's been going for 20 years. They've got around 100

different manufacturers listed on their website and reckon to be able to help out with parts.

Or try www.partmaster.co.uk (part of the Dixons, Currys group) but shop around; manufacturers will usually quote a price inclusive of delivery but parts can take around 10 days to reach you whereas some of the other websites may be more expensive but you're usually paying for next-day delivery.

China/Porcelain Repair

For quick repairs of chipped mugs or vases you can buy something called Milliput. It comes in different grades and colours and costs around a fiver. You get a two-part epoxy system, which has a long shelf life. Cut off equal parts of each and knead them together for about five minutes to mix well. Then use to build up and repair over chips, or to fix together broken pieces. This works really well and hardens in a few hours when it can be sanded, drilled or whatever. It's dishwasher safe and can withstand temperatures up to 150°C.

If you've chipped your best china but don't want to throw away the set try www.lostpottery.co.uk for new and second-hand replacements. They tend to stock the posher china so you won't find M&S or Boots own lines there – more like Wedgwood and Royal Doulton – but they've got stocks of china going back 30 years or so. If it's a replacement cup and saucer or vegetable dish you're after, check them out. Prices start at around £10 for second-hand pieces. And if you're looking to flog off a spare set of china, see if they'll buy it off you.

Gardens

Patios and Paths

◆ Clean patio stones covered with moss with a bucket of bleach and warm water mixed half and half. Pour it on and brush with a stiff brush – or use Jeyes fluid washed down with water.

◆ Put a generous squeeze or two of bleach into a watering can, fill it up with cold water and water the patio. It doesn't need to be rinsed off. The rain seems to clear it and after a day or two the patio comes up really bright. Saves scrubbing with a yard brush.

Weedkiller

◆ Water down some Jeyes fluid and put it into a spray gun to spray round the garden.

◆ This can also be used to deter creepy crawlies from getting in the house if sprayed round the outside. Don't use if you have pets as it can be very toxic to animals.

◆ You can also make your own with one cup of vinegar and half a cup of washing-up liquid. Put in a spray bottle and top up with water.

◆ You can use white vinegar straight from the bottle or salt (buy the big tubs of cooking salt) sprinkled over the weeds.

Sheds

◆ To get rid of green algae on sheds and fence panels, wash down with a half-and-half bleach and hot water solution. Other algae-busting methods include washing down with some washing soda (about 56p *a pack in the supermarket) or using hot water with biological washing powder and scrubbing with a stiff brush.*

Wheelie Bins

◆   *To get rid of maggots and creepy crawlies from the bottom of the bin pour on a mug of salt to kill them.*

◆   *Loads of companies out there will come round to clean out your bin for a fee but for a cheap Old-Style alternative just throw in some soapy water and clean out with a hard bristle broom. Or get some cheap disinfectant (35p Asda Smart Price for a 1 litre bottle), pour it in, swill round and then pour out over the drain. Never throw anything in your bins that's not carefully bagged up.*

Car Maintenance and Cleaning

◆   *Clean the inside of the windows with scrunched-up newspaper and a squirt of vinegar.*

◆   *For screen wash, you can fill up the washer bottle with warm water and a squirt of washing-up liquid, though it's not too good for the paintwork so shouldn't be used as a long-term solution. Asda and Morrisons sell budget-priced screen wash for around £1 rather than the more expensive stuff from Halfords.*

◆   *For unsightly oil stains on the driveway, sprinkle over some cat litter, leave overnight and sweep away. The cat litter absorbs most of the oil.*

◆   *To get rid of horrid sticker marks on car windows or mess left by car park tickets, spray with WD40 and wipe away.*

◆ *To clean up leather car upholstery, try baby wipes or saddle soap (about £1.50 a bar from 'country' shops), dampen a sponge, rub on the soap and rub into the leather. Wipe dry with an old towel. Keeps the leather supple too.*

◆ *With repairs, try getting parts from scrap yards to keep the cost down if it's a job that can be done at home. The same goes for older models where parts may be harder to get hold of and involve ordering direct from the manufacturer.*

◆ *Taking a basic evening class course in car maintenance can save heaps of cash in the long run. The average cost of a service can be around £100 upwards so if you've got the know-how to change spark plugs, change the oil and replace the air filter and so on you can easily recoup the costs. Borrow a car manual from the library for added back-up.*

Sprucing Up Your House For Sale

You must have seen at least one of those property/DIY programmes on television. If not, here's a quick reminder of the oft-touted selling and 'kerb-appeal' techniques.

◆ *When viewers come round make sure that your house is clean and fresh, bright and quiet. This may involve giving some shabby walls a lick of warm, neutral paint; using air fresheners; displaying fresh flowers and playing soothing music.*

◆ *Slightly more strenuous, but equally important, tasks include finally* fitting those spotlights you've had sitting in the lounge since you moved in and painting the fence. All this will make the property more welcoming and help viewers picture themselves in your home.

◆ And if television makeover shows are to be believed, remember you're selling a 'lifestyle' that people will aspire to, so spread a few glossy magazines around (borrow from friends) and get that fresh filter coffee brewing.

◆ For an instant air freshener, stick a fabric softener sheet in the bathroom waste paper basket to give the room a nice smell.

◆ Check out the cleaning chapter for more advice on quick and cheap ways to get your house clean in super-quick time.

◆ Finish off small DIY jobs like touching up chipped paint on the woodwork and replacing washers on dripping taps.

◆ By the time your buyers have got to the front door they've already formed an opinion so make sure the front lawn's been mown, the path is tidy and the gate isn't falling off its hinges.

◆ You might love your photos but prospective buyers might see them as clutter. Try and tidy everything away and go for a minimalist look when buyers visit.

◆ Sticking a few healthy plants around the house and even fresh flowers are all little cosmetic touches that go a long way.

◆ Don't cook up a curry the night before; stale food odours are horrid. If the house smells, stick a bowl of white vinegar in the corner of the room or burn some scented candles. Or if you've really got into the Old-Style spirit, freshly bake some bread!

Chapter 5

THE GOOD LIFE - GROW YOUR OWN

It's often cheaper – and definitely easier – to buy unhealthy food than to stock up on fresh fruit and vegetables. Sticking a frozen pizza and bag of chips in your trolley can cost next to nothing compared with buying fresh food, so if you want those five portions of fresh fruit and veg without making a dent in your bank balance why not get out there, kit yourself out in a pair of wellies and grow your own!

This chapter includes information on what to grow and where to grow it, finding an allotment (if your own back garden's non-existent) and, if you want to take your self-sufficiency that one step further, how to keep your own ducks and hens.

GETTING STARTED WITH GROWING YOUR OWN

When it comes to *what* to grow it makes sense to start with something you enjoy eating lots of, so while you might pick up some radish seeds on the cheap, if you hardly eat the things all your hard efforts in the garden will go to waste.

Start with the basics like potatoes, tomatoes, carrots and ideally something you can grow fairly cheaply from a few peelings or pips.

◆ *If you want to buy seeds, avoid garden centres as they tend to be really expensive. Go somewhere like Lidl where you can pick up packs for around 30p. Wilkinson and Poundstretcher are also good sources of cheap seeds, and there are loads of websites like www.alanromans.com which sells veggie seeds at around 50p a packet.*

◆ *Don't buy pots and containers for home growing. Save up all your old yoghurt pots, margarine tubs, ready-meal trays and the plastic boxes you get at the deli in Costco for seed planting. These are great for starting things off on the windowsill, but if you're going to keep them outside uncovered watch out on windy days!*

◆ *For cheap but bigger growing containers ask your local flower shop if they've got any spare black plastic flower buckets or try Asda. They've usually got holes in the bottom already so they're great for water drainage, and you can grow pretty much anything in them, either in the garden or on an allotment.*

◆ *Ask round locally about 'seed exchange events' where you can go and swap seeds with other local gardeners. A real bonus to this is there's lots of free advice on hand, as well as the chance to swap your spare seeds for something different.*

Think Small to Start

◆   *You don't need lots of growing space. Start with spinach and salad in
    some old plastic salad containers (Asda or Tesco). Stick them on the
    windowsill to ensure they get as much sunlight as possible. And
    carrots, onions and peppers can be grown in similar pots and tubs
    until they're big enough to be transferred outside.*

◆   *Start by filling the containers with a layer of gravel or broken up
    polystyrene (if you've got some) and then top up with compost.*

◆   *Start off seeds in cardboard egg cartons; once they have grown and
    are ready for replanting just stick the whole thing into compost as the
    cardboard will decompose over time.*

◆   *Make your own compost – old rotting banana skins and teabags are
    ideal. Or you can use banana skins to boost your roses by sticking
    them around the roses just under the soil surface.*

◆   *The 'innards' of toilet rolls can be used for growing beans, peas and
    sweet peas.*

◆   *Plant labels are easy to make from strips of old plastic milk cartons.*

◆   *And don't chuck out old laddered tights – they make great plant
    ties.*

◆   *Cut down plastic soft drink bottles (2 litre ones are best) to make
    cheap cloche plant protectors to look after small plants and act as
    mini greenhouses.*

◆   *Buy some plain cheap cat litter and mix it with compost for hanging
    baskets; it helps absorb water and prevents the baskets drying out –
    you can of course buy commercial granules for the job but cat litter's
    a fraction of the price.*

◆ *If you've got one of those big round bins and it's tall enough to stop dogs getting in, try growing stuff in it. Potatoes grow well in here.*

◆ *Make or get hold of an old wooden box – you can grow garlic, baby carrots, chives, thyme, mint, lemon grass and sage in it.*

What Should I Grow?

A quick straw poll on the Old-Style boards reveals garlic, lettuce, rocket, tomatoes and strawberries as the easiest and most popular fruit and veg to grow for the complete garden novice.

Tomatoes
Can be grown from pips – scoop them out from an old tomato, dry them on a piece of kitchen roll and they'll be ready for planting the next day, or buy small plants cheap at the village fête. They'll need a bit of warmth to help them grow so if you haven't got a greenhouse let them grow against a wall in a sheltered spot. The easiest way is to get a grow bag or you can just plant them in ordinary old compost.

Strawberries
Always a good one to grow as they tend to be pricey in the shops and still seem a bit 'luxurious'. They can be planted in grow bags and reproduce like rabbits, with loads more plants every year. Easy to freeze for puddings and jam making and not much hassle to grow.

Rhubarb

This is great value and easy to grow. Buy or scrounge a 'crown', then all you have to do is leave it a year to build up some strength and every year after you'll get a rhubarb harvest. Keep pulling some of it up so you don't get overwhelmed.

Lettuce

Keep a lookout for slugs and snails. They love lettuce and can wreck your whole crop. Easy to start off in pots and then replant or leave in pots in the garden.

Potatoes

A staple for any allotment or garden and easy to grow, regardless of whatever has been grown there before, and you get loads for very little effort. You can even start them off from old potato peelings or potatoes that have started to 'sprout', though you'll generally get smaller potatoes than if you'd grown them from seed.

All you need is an old bucket or dustbin with some holes drilled around the sides about two inches up from the base. Put some small pebbles in up to the holes. Then stick in some compost, either bought or home-made (don't use soil as it will dry rock hard), and put the sprouting potatoes, peelings or seeds on the compost. Cover with more compost. This will only be about halfway up the container. When the leaves grow and are clear of the surface add more compost and keep filling it up as the stalks get higher. When the foliage starts to die off in mid- to late summer, tip them out and eat.

Grow Your Own Herbs

Basil, coriander, chives, parsley, thyme – all ideal for growing on the windowsill. A few pots are needed (remember those old margarine tubs?), a handful of compost and pick up some cheap seeds at the supermarket (Wilkinsons or anywhere where they're doing three-for-two type offers). Herb seeds have been spotted in Lidl for around 20p a packet.

And garlic's even easier – just stick a couple of cloves in a pot to grow your own. They can be planted outdoors during spring and summer or grown indoors all year round near sunny windows.

For more ideas on what to grow check out the Old-Style index thread at www.moneysavingexpert.com/osgrowyourown

ALLOTMENTS

If your back garden's the size of a postage stamp you can get away with growing most things in pots and window boxes, but if you want more space it's worth thinking about getting an allotment. No longer just for little old men, a.k.a. *EastEnders*' 'Arthur Fowler' or the 'flat cap' brigade, the fastest-growing group of allotment holders are women under 40. And in Manchester there's been a 20 per cent increase in the number of allotment gardeners under 30 over the last five years.

Quick History of Allotments

Allotments date back some 200 years. The word 'allotment' originates from land being 'allotted' to an individual under an enclosure award (enclosures tended to be used by rich landowners to stop the poor grazing their animals on common land). With the onset of the Industrial Revolution, many people moved to the towns to work in the factories and, with food becoming both scarce and expensive, turned to growing their own.

During World War I there was a huge growth in the number of allotments, from around half a million to over one-and-a-half million. During the world wars many parks were turned into allotments, but when wartime rationing ended many allotments went into decline.

Not surprisingly, the new-found popularity for allotments is mainly due to public concern over the quality of food and the desire to live a healthier lifestyle.

Finding an Allotment

An allotment is more than just an extra garden; it's a whole new lifestyle. With it often come new friends, advice, healthy living and food that is clean, wholesome and cheap. And don't underestimate the fitness benefits either – it's cheaper than gym membership.

Word of mouth is always a great starting point to finding an allotment, but if you don't know anyone who's got one start by contacting your local authority, either your parish or town council, where information should be available on potential sites. Or ask at your local library for details of allotment associations. Don't expect to go down armed with your spade and seeds straight away as the more popular sites can have long waiting lists, often a year or more.

What Size Should I Get?

A full 'plot' is usually 250 square metres (16 metres by 16 metres). As a very rough guide, this is about enough to supply a family of four with vegetables all year round, but half plots are usually available if this is too much. You'll usually pay an annual ground rent to use the allotment, and prices vary. One Old-Styler claimed to find one for £2.50 a year but this really is 'dirt(!)' cheap judging by the astonished response he got. The average cost tends to be around £35 a year.

Questions to Ask

◆ *Check what facilities are available – most allotments have running water but it's worth checking. Find out if there's any storage, such as a shed, where you can leave your tools, and if there are any toilets on the site.*

◆ *It's also worth asking if there are any restrictions in the lease. For example, are you forbidden to plant fruit trees or put up a greenhouse?*

◆ *Check out the Old-Style index thread at www.moneysavingexpert.com/ osallotments for more tips or contact the National Society of Allotment and Leisure Gardeners www.nsalg.or.uk*

Planning Your Planting

Make a list of all the fruit and veg you enjoy. Ask your neighbours (either allotment or garden) whether they've had any problems with particular crops due to the soil conditions or local pests like slugs or badgers. Don't get too disheartened because your garden or allotment doesn't look like a show garden after the first year; it can take time to get it in good growing order.

It's worth trying to extend the harvest season by using a layer of fleece (try your local market) over your crops; this way you can get a long harvest of spinach, rocket and lettuce in the autumn as it's mainly the rain and wind damage that finish things off before the frost kicks in. Sow the seeds at the end of July so you have little plants to put in your protected bed by the middle of September. And think how smug you can feel taking home your salads in November!

FARMERS' MARKETS

Having started in California, farmers' markets have been big in the States for over 40 years and they're really catching on over here too with over 500 taking place regularly across the UK. Not only are you guaranteed fresh produce but buying from a farmers' market means you're also supporting your local economy. As many markets are only held once a week, many farms are now starting their own farm shops or organic food box schemes. Check out www.farmersmarkets.net for a list of markets and shops in your area.

Don't assume farmers' markets are cheaper than the supermarkets, though the produce is usually organic, and they should be cheaper than supermarkets' organic ranges as they're more locally produced. Plus many believe the produce has fuller flavour, so you can buy less.

◆ *To get the best bargains find out what time the market's open and head down shortly before closing. Most stall holders will be selling off produce they can't keep fresh.*

◆ *You'll often get a free feed as many stall holders are generous with their samples like cheese, bread and pickles, so it's great for a cheap brunch too.*

◆ *Most farms have 'pick your own' days, cheaper once again than buying at the supermarket — check local farms, local papers and sites like www.bigbarn.co.uk for details.*

FREE FOOD

The hedgerows and land of Britain has a lot of food going for free. Do check you know exactly what you're picking though.

Blackberries

Pick your own from hedgerows but avoid any too low on the ground as the dogs might have visited them first! Wash them in a bowl with water and a quarter of a mug of white vinegar to kill the germs; soak for half an hour before drying and storing or using.

There are loads of blackberry recipes in the Old-Style index thread. For other 'hedgerow' recipes try www.overthegardengate.net for, among others, rosehip jelly, nettle soup and elderberry wine.

Elderberries

Great for making cordial, ice cream, jelly and pies. Here's a quick recipe.

Blackberry and Elderberry Jam
Take equal quantities of blackberries and elderberries (stripped of stalks), put in a pan, bring to the boil and cook for 20 minutes. Allow 340g (12oz) of sugar to each 455g (1lb) of fruit, bring to the boil for 20 minutes, cool and put in jars.

Rosehips

Use to make rosehip syrup or jelly and as a remedy for coughs, colds and flu. Once picked, mix with sugar, boil up, cool and put in jars. Add a teaspoon to boiling water to make a 'tea'.

Nettles

Remember to wear gloves when picking, though nettles don't sting when cooked! Nettles are said to be very rich in nutrients but don't gather them beside roads where they will have been contaminated by traffic fumes. If you have them in your garden and keep cutting them you get a regular supply of fresh leaves.

Nettle Soup   *Serves 6*

1 onion, chopped
2 cloves of garlic, chopped
2 tbsp oil
3 handfuls of freshly picked and washed young nettles
3 tbsp flour
500ml (1 pint) soya milk
500ml (1 pint) water or stock
Salt and pepper to taste

Fry the onion and garlic in the oil for a few minutes then stir in the nettles until soft. Stir in the flour and gradually add the soya milk and water or stock, stirring all the time. Add seasoning and liquidise.

Wild Garlic

Found in damp woods and hedge banks but don't use once they've finished flowering as the leaves can be a bit tough. Leaves can be used in salads or sauces and you can chop them to use in soured cream or mayonnaise. For a great sauce for roast lamb or a barbecue dip, liquidise two handfuls of wild garlic leaves, some olive oil and capers. Store in the fridge. You can also use the leaves in home-made quiches.

HOUSEHOLD PESTS

There's an array of sprays and potions to get rid of household pests; here's how to do the job without setting foot in the DIY store.

Ant Killer

◆ *Old-Style myth has it that they won't cross heavy chalk or peppermint oil so try putting some down outside their hole.*
◆ *Spray affected areas with a mix of tea tree oil and water.*
◆ *Cayenne pepper near their holes is also supposed to deter them.*
◆ *Or try chilli powder for the same effect.*
◆ *Or even sprinkling sage.*
◆ *And for the outside of the house, neat white vinegar sprayed on the outside of the windowsills and rubbed dry with newspaper repels them.*

Fly Killer

- *Make your own fly paper using 55g (2oz) of syrup (any kind of sticky stuff – golden syrup will do), 1 tbsp of brown sugar and 1 tbsp of granulated sugar. Mix the ingredients together in a small bowl and pour over strips of brown paper and leave to soak overnight. To hang, poke a hole in one end of a strip and tie a string to it.*
- *Honey smeared on double-sided sticky tape and stuck on the window gathers them within seconds (but you might need to do a spot of window cleaning afterwards unless you're careful!)*
- *Growing lavender and basil in pots near windows can deter them.*
- *No fly spray? Use hairspray instead for the same effect.*

Mosquitoes

Can ruin any summer's evening. To get rid of them stick a piece of stinky blue cheese at the other side of the garden; they love the stuff and will flock round it leaving you alone to enjoy your evening.

Taking vitamin B tablets or eating heaps of Marmite (on toast) can work for some people but if you do get bitten, a dab of white vinegar is heralded by the Old-Style as a wonder cure, but the stuff stinks so don't go too mad.

Wasps

Get a tall jar or vase and put some honey or jam in the bottom with some water. Make a paper lid with a hole cut in it (make the hole quite generous). The idea is that the wasps will be attracted by the sweet smell, fly in but then can't get out. Ideal to stick around the patio on summer days or during picnics. Empty every day.

Moths

Clean out the inside of wardrobes with a white vinegar and water solution. And put a cloth with a small amount of tea tree oil on it at the back of the wardrobe too.

Slugs

They hate rough surfaces so crushing up some eggshells and sticking them near wherever they're getting in is worth a go. Can be a bit messy and time consuming as you'll need to vacuum up the shells the next morning. Or set a trap by getting a cut-down plastic drink bottle with a small amount of something sweet like cola in the bottom. Prop it up a little so the slugs get in but can't get out.

KEEPING LIVESTOCK

Keeping chickens is a major Old-Style pastime: nothing beats fresh eggs every morning from your own hens. While cows and pigs are a bit out of your league if you've got the average-sized back garden, chickens and ducks are probably the easiest livestock to take on. Goats have a tendency to eat pretty much everything and can be quite destructive but chickens are easy to look after, entertaining and very good value when it comes to eating up the scraps and some of the garden pests, like slugs.

Chickens

On the plus side you'll (hopefully) get a constant supply of fresh eggs, which makes the hens a very good long-term investment. Downside? If you're proud of your beautifully manicured lawns think twice; hens can ruin your grass. They love to dig around and bathe in the dust so it's unlikely anything apart from established bushes like roses or maybe mint will survive. Naturally they'll need a home so you'll need to make or buy a hen house for them.

Day to day they're not too much harder to look after than any other pets in terms of feeding them but you've really got to be around every day to let them out in the morning, collect the eggs and get them in at night.

What Sort of Hens Do I Buy?

Before you rush out and buy a couple of hens from your nearest farm, it's worth checking your house deeds to ensure there are no restrictions on keeping livestock, as in some cases there may be a clause that prevents this.

If all that's okay then you've got to think about what breed to buy. The good news is you can mix and match breeds pretty much problem-free. Black Rocks tend to be the Old-Style favourite as they're supposed to be 'bomb proof' and aren't scared off by cats and dogs – a fair enough reason if you've already got a family pet.

Cost-wise, a lot depends on where you live and where you're buying. As a rough guide for fully vaccinated 'point of lay' hens (typically around 18 weeks old) bought from a registered supplier, you can expect to pay around £5–£8 a bird. But you can also buy them as cheaply as £1 a bird from farmers' markets, although sometimes the cheaper ones are ex-battery hens. Their average lifespan is around four to five years, and they tend to lay fewer eggs the older they get.

Where to Buy?

Your best bet is a local market or farmer who has free-range hens; but you can also try county fairs or local poultry shows, which are bound to be advertised locally, and it's always worth a trawl on the net. Try the RSPCA, free ads or spend a couple of hours in 'Smiths' reading magazines like *Practical Poultry*. You don't have to buy the magazine; just write down the breeders' contact numbers and call them when you get home.

Some of the Old-Style community have bought 'spent' or 'end of lay' hens from local farmers. They'll need a little TLC at first but you can still get eggs from them. Many Old-Stylers have even bought ex-battery hens as cheaply as 50 pence each; on the plus side not only are they being re-homed but many lay eggs at a rate of knots. For those interested in re-homing ex-battery hens contact www.thehenshouse.co.uk

Before You Get Started

Think about how many hens you want (ideally aim to keep at least three), and it's best to get them together as it can be hard to add to a flock later, especially for beginners.

Where are you going to keep them? Grass is the best surface, but if you're restricted to a patio or paved area then a layer of straw or bark will give them something to rummage around on. They do tend to peck around somewhat and they're more than likely to scratch up new seedlings and plants; they'll dig in the vegetable patch and even have a go at the compost heap; as mentioned earlier, though, established shrubs should be okay.

If you keep chickens on the same ground for a long time, parasites build up. It's generally recommended that when they've ruined the ground, you move their run so the ground can recover. This is the idea behind those self-contained arks and coops with small runs attached; you move it round every few days so the ground gets a rest while the chickens get fresh grass.

For more information on buying and keeping chickens take a look at www.smallholder.co.uk

Chicken Coops

First up you'll need a small shed or coop for them to sleep in at night and lay eggs in. They'll need protection against foxes so some sort of covered run is essential. If you're looking to buy rather than make your own, you can get some very trendy-looking hen houses known as 'Eglus' from www.omlet.co.uk. They look fantastic but cost around £350 (though the price does include two chickens, fencing and a kind of starter pack). A cheaper alternative is to get a second-hand shed and screw in a couple of home-made perches about a foot from the floor. Bed down with straw and place a couple of those shallow, wooden fruit crates at the back with straw in for a DIY comfy chicken house.

The ideal size you'll need is around 1 metre square for about eight hens. Their house must be well-ventilated and dark. Generally the bigger the space they've got the better as they can bully one another badly if kept in cramped conditions.

You can even convert an old unused kids' playhouse to a chicken coop and just add on a fenced run yourself. If you're doing this then put wood shavings on the floor and make some sort of perch packed with loads of straw or get some nest boxes. Try free ads or farmers or even ask the neighbours for old sheds if you're stuck. If you're making a run make sure the fencing goes right to the ground as chickens can squeeze themselves through any small gaps to make their bid for freedom!

Upkeep

Once a week you'll need to clean them out. Get rid of the mucky straw on the compost heap, put some clean stuff down and, once a month, give the whole house a really good scrub down. Hens aren't noisy creatures like cockerels so they shouldn't be waking the kids and neighbours every morning.

When it comes to what they eat, that's pretty much anything and everything. For an exhaustive list check out www.moneysavingexpert.com/oschickens

Don't bother spending your money buying special chicken feed. Just feed them on scraps and leftovers. Here are some of the top-rated Old-Style chicken dinners:

◆ *Potato peelings*
◆ *Apple cores*
◆ *Slugs*
◆ *Porridge*
◆ *Bits of cheese*
◆ *Breadcrumbs*
◆ *Cooked pasta (leftovers)*
◆ *Cooked rice (ditto)*
◆ *Carrot peelings*
◆ *Nuts (hazelnuts left over from Christmas)*
◆ *Cabbage leaves*
◆ *Lettuce trimmings*
◆ *Sweetcorn husks*
◆ *Melon and kiwi fruit peel (they don't eat it but they strip it clean, same for the sweetcorn)*

REAL OLD-STYLE STORY

Mine can be a bit fussy when it comes to food but they do like tea and orange juice – straight from our cups if we leave them. They love flies and ants and run a mile to catch a daddy-longlegs!

Eggs

Hens tend to lay the most eggs in their first year, and egg production decreases gradually year by year. The typical 'egg-laying' season tends to be between April and October but don't expect as many eggs if it's excessively hot.

As a rough rule of thumb you can reckon on between 100 to 300 eggs a year per bird. Work out the cost of your chickens and divide it by the cost of a box of eggs; this gives you the approximate number of weeks' 'lay' that it will take to recoup your investment.

Ducks

More messy than hens and not to be bought simply because you have an idyllic image of a couple of nice-looking ducks on your garden pond. The reality is that within a week it will be a stinking mess!

Ducks also love digging holes in lawns, so if you want a perfect lawn, no ducks. They shoot poo everywhere as well as in water so be prepared for a lot of clearing up. Food-wise they can eat pretty much the same as chickens so you don't need to shell out on extra food. The eggs need more cleaning up than chicken eggs do – some warm water and a damp cloth should do the trick.

Popular breeds for first-time smallholders are the Indian Runner and the Khaki Campbell.

Where to Buy?

Look in the back of *The Smallholder* magazine or search on the Internet; as with hens, ask at local farms or check for adverts in local papers. Price-wise, once again it varies according to where you buy but around £10 a duck is a very rough average cost.

And if you've got spare eggs the cheapest way to sell them is to stick a sign on your front door or on your local town or village notice board; anywhere that doesn't cost too much money to advertise.

For more information about keeping livestock go to the Old-Style index thread at www.moneysavingexpert.com/oslivestock

REAL OLD-STYLE STORY

I used to help out with functions such as weddings and christenings. At the end of the night I would go round and chuck all the leftover buffet (salad, pasta, bread rolls, fruit salad, sandwiches . . . anything) in a black bag for my Mum's hens.

The following morning I would empty a FULL bin liner of goodies into the chicken run. You've never seen such happy ex-battery hens in your life. If any of you know any caterers then get in there with your bin bags.

Chapter 6

PRESENTS AND HOME-MADE GIFTS

Don't shell out on those tiresome and pointless presents we often all give and receive come Christmas and birthdays. Home-made gifts are much more affordable and the sentiment's more appreciated than a shop-bought present.

And anyone of a certain age who was once given, or made, what was probably the ultimate 'Blue Peter' Christmas present – an orange stuffed with cloves turned smelly pomander – will know the effort that goes into home-made presents and how sentimental they can be.

This chapter's all about being resourceful, never having to make a last-minute dash to the shops and blowing your budget because you can't find the perfect gift. It's about how to make your own, and if you haven't got a creative bone in your body, how to shop all year round to build up the perfect gift cupboard for every occasion. It's about how to recycle presents, and how to save a fortune on all the wrapping and trimmings that can often boost the cost of present buying by around a fiver.

So to get started here's how to turn your hand to making home-made cards the easy way.

HOME-MADE CARDS

Pick up any card in Clintons or any of the high-street shops and you can easily pay around £2 and add on a couple of quid more if it's got just a touch of 'hand-made' about it with little ribbons or stick-on bits and glitter. In the UK we spend a whopping £1 billion on cards a year, the third most popular purchase after chocolate bars and cola.

One of the easiest ways to make cards is on a computer. Okay, there are plenty of websites where you can download and send free email cards, but nothing beats the real thing. You can personalise birthday cards for friends and family using, say, pictures of their favourite film stars, cartoons, pictures or photos, and get creative adding personalised text or speech bubbles with 'personal messages'.

Foolproof Computer Cards

Here's how to make a basic card template on the computer.

- *Create a landscape document in Word or something similar.*
- *Divide the page up into four quarters. You can use the on-screen guides to get it right.*
- *The bottom-right quadrant will be the front of the card. Paste your downloaded or scanned image and text in this bit.*
- *The upper-left quadrant is the inside of the card. Here you can write your greeting, but you'll have to paste the text box upside down because the card's unfolded as yet.*

- *Print off the A4 sheet on thin card, and fold it in half horizontally then in half again vertically, giving you a card with the picture on the front and the greeting inside.*
- *You may need to trial and error this a few times so use scrap paper to start.*

Card-making Supplies

Save everything in the way of coloured card, tissue paper, glitter, ribbon, pictures from magazines, old photos, anything that comes your way and buy any other bits you need in stores like Hobbycraft. To pick up some savvy card-making tips it's worth spending a couple of afternoons in front of the television watching the QVC channel (if you can get it) as they often have 'crafting days'. The kits they sell can be expensive but you can adapt their ideas to make your own. Or if you can't find any creative card-making shows then borrow some books from the local library.

- *You've made the cards but what about the envelopes? Buy coloured ones cheaply in places like Woolies where you can pick up packs of 20 for a couple of pounds.*
- *It's worth trying shops that sell kids' art supplies as the cutting and sticking stuff can often be cheaper. Save everything in a 'cutting and sticking' box.*
- *If you know anyone who's a dressmaker, ask them for offcuts of material, especially if they make wedding dresses – great for luxury beading that can be pricey.*

- *Pressed flowers can look great on cards but don't bother buying expensive flower presses – just put a pile of your heaviest books on top of them.*
- *Hang on to any card designs you like so you can copy them.*
- *Children usually love making their own cards so if they've got birthdays coming up for friends at school, encourage them to make their own.*

GIFTS

Whatever the occasion, whether it's an impending birthday, wedding anniversary or colleague's last day at work, panic present buying is horrid. It usually means you end up with the wrong thing in a mad haste to buy 'something', and you spend more than you wanted to because you haven't time to shop around. Having an all-year-round, any-occasion 'gift cupboard' saves stress and cash on unexpected party invitations for the kids or family birthdays you've forgotten.

Start a Gift Cupboard

- *Whenever you're shopping and spot something that would make a good present, buy it. All those 'three for two' offers, BOGOFs and sale items can be stored up to save cash come birthdays and Christmas. Though don't go OTT – keep it in proportion.*
- *You can stick anything and everything in the gift cupboard. Start with*

plain cards (that can double up as birthday, moving house and so on) and any-occasion rolls of gift wrap.

◆ Add duplicate toys, so if one of the children gets two of something, stick one in the gift cupboard for another party.

◆ Recycle gifts. There's nothing wrong with passing on unwanted gifts to others (providing you take off the gift tag!) Remember who gave it to you in the first place so you don't get caught out giving it back!

◆ Keep a notebook to hand with a list of who you buy for during the year and what you've got in the prezzie cupboard. This way you'll always have something for every occasion and a few spares.

◆ Check your prezzie cupboard or box from time to time. There's no point buying loads of bargain bits only to find chocolates that are out of date, so try to use up anything with a limited shelf life before buying more.

◆ All those sachets of shampoo, foundation and moisturiser and even lipsticks that come free with magazines can be put in a make-up bag and given as a gift come Mother's Day or birthdays. And decanting favourite moisturisers and bubble baths into those cheap plastic pots and containers you can buy in the pound shop means you've got an instant 'travel' pack for a present.

Don't get too organised and wrap everything too early or you could have a problem remembering what's what. Either put tags on them or, if you're not sure who's getting them yet, just stick a small picture on each one or you'll spend hours unwrapping and rewrapping them.

Storage-wise, those cheap plastic storage crates usually found in kids' rooms are great, or keep all the gifts in a special present drawer, hidden away from small fingers and prying eyes!

Having built up your gift cupboard, don't be tempted to start giving them away unnecessarily during the year or handing them out when the kids are bored in the summer holidays or rainy Sunday afternoons, otherwise it becomes a costly rather than a thrifty exercise.

REAL OLD-STYLE STORY

I always kept a present box when the children were younger. Both were in classes of 20 and through primary school seemed to have a birthday party a week, so whenever I saw items at bargain prices I'd get it for the present box.

January was a great time for stocking up as the supermarkets have clearouts of all their Christmas presents. I also had a box of assorted value and cheap cards and some sticky numbers to put on them, and I bought large value rolls of wrapping paper that would be suitable for boy or girl. This way I was never caught out by 'Mum, it's Jack/Jane's party today and I forgot to give you the invite'.

Make Your Own Gift Hampers

Come Christmas you can't move for shop shelves laden with all those 'gift' packs and hampers. It's a great way for the stores to bundle up a load of stuff and sell it at double the price just because it's in pretty packaging. And if you've ever bought one, whether it's tea and jams or cosmetics, chances are there are always some bits in there that won't get used, so why not make your own?

'Home' Hampers

◆ *Make a craft kit – get a cheap photo frame, varnish, glue and unusual things to decorate the frame, and package it all up in a box or basket from the pound shop, market or in one you had from a previous present.*

◆ *Buy some glass jars and layer up with Epsom salts, dried rose petals and essential oils – costs next to nothing and looks good. You can pick up glass jars and bottles fairly cheaply in markets or pound shops; even IKEA does some budget-priced kitchen-style glass jars and pots that can be used for this. Add a pretty box to look as good as the shop-bought ones.*

◆ *A nice pot for the garden with a miniature tree or plant like a bay tree, magnolia or eucalyptus looks good. Buy a glazed pot and decorate it yourself with stuck-on glass beads.*

Food Hampers

◆   How's this for a leaving present for a work colleague? A mug, teaspoon, sachets of coffee and hot chocolate, chocolate bars and maybe a lolly all wrapped up in pretty cellophane with some of those confetti-style sprinkles around it?

◆   And you can adapt the idea for a 'chocoholic' if you can resist the temptation to eat it first! Get loads of sachets of hot chocolate; buy some bars of chocolate in the local market (they often have deals like 10 bars for a pound) and put a few marshmallows in it; tie it all up in cellophane (buy cheap at the florist) and stick a nice bow on the top – just like the sort of thing you get in Boots or Whittards but cheaper.

◆   Kids will love their own baking set – write out or print some easy recipes for cookies and muffins, add the ingredients and cutters, things to stick on them and maybe a kids' rolling pin and apron (with their name embroidered on it). Use a mixing bowl as the hamper container; supermarkets have inexpensive colourful plastic salad bowls that look better than the plain white or cream ones.

◆   Home-made chocolates, jams, cakes, muffins, cookies, lemon curd, flapjacks . . . Home-made goodies make great presents. Buy an inexpensive flatpack gift box (or ask your local bakery for some), line with a doily or tissue paper before putting the goodies in or do the all-American thing and display them in a basket, complete with checked tea towel on top, just like Bree from Desperate Housewives.

REAL OLD-STYLE STORY

Make a 'Wedding Night Survival Box' – with a bottle of bubbly, a tube of Pringles, pack of chocolate Hobnobs, some posh nibbles, a large bottle of water and some strawberries, in a mini cool bag. I covered that with more tissue paper (the top of the bubbly peeping out) and laid two cheapo champagne flutes on top, tied together with a bit of pretty ribbon, and connived with the hotel to have it delivered to their room with two buckets of ice.

I reckon it cost me about £20 all in but it could be done for a great deal less than that fairly easily.

Wedding Presents

◆ *If you're a good photographer, take some informal black-and-white shots and put them in a nice album or take loads of photos at the evening party (they're the ones the official photographer often misses or isn't there for) and put together a fun album to go with the 'official' one.*

◆ *Another idea that can be really personal is to gather together lots of quotes about marriage, love, living together, sharing and so on, and make a nice book with them in – either practise your calligraphy skills or print them out on the computer.*

- ◆ You can easily make a souvenir box with memories of the day, like a newspaper from the day of the wedding, the cork from the champagne, a slice of cake, the confetti, order of service and so on.
- ◆ Or invent your own 'marriage survival kit' – be as rude as you dare! You could include romantic books, wine, board games, or get each guest to write a line of advice on a card and put that in.

For loads more ideas for gift hampers, go to the Old-Style index thread at www.moneysavingexpert.com/osgifthamper

'Green' Gifts

Don't want to buy a 'gift' or not sure what to give? Check out the online Fairtrade shops or sponsor an animal like one of those 'buy a cow' or 'give a goat' schemes. Or go practical and buy a compost bin or energy-saving light bulbs. And if you're remotely creative, paint some old flower pots and planters; you can use spray paint or even plain old emulsion, and they should last even outdoors for up to a couple of years. Don't buy new tins of paint; mix up a concoction from the leftovers you've got kicking around in the garden shed. Those huge terracotta-style planters look good but can be expensive at the garden centre; for a cheaper version buy up some cheap plastic tubs, paint them with plain yoghurt (yes you did read that right!), put them in the sun and within a couple of weeks they'll have that 'weathered' terracotta look.

Other Gifts

◆ Buy cheap glassware (like Tesco value wine glasses or tumblers) and decorate with special 'glass paints' and pens from hobby stores. The finished versions are the sort of thing sold at craft fairs for quite a bit.

◆ You can spend loads of money on those 'gift experience' days so make your own by organising a day to the coast or find some free museums. You could organise a walk to somewhere with special memories; if it's your mum or dad take them on a tour of their old childhood haunts, the house they grew up in, first school and so on, and make a nice card to present it.

◆ For someone moving home, adapt the gift hamper idea to make a 'new home' box – include both practical and fun things, say a torch, bottle of wine, corkscrew, mugs, tea bags, biscuits, batteries and so on.

◆ For big number birthdays or wedding anniversaries, make photo collage boards. Literally beg, borrow and steal loads of snaps from over the years, arrange and stick them on a large piece of cardboard in a haphazard fashion along with anything else of sentimental value, such as tickets for a theatre show they loved, and put the whole thing in a clip frame from Woolies or IKEA.

◆ Take some cuttings from one of your favourite plants, grow them for a bit and wrap up.

◆ Swap your Tesco vouchers for presents; you can get up to four times the value if you trade them in rather than use them as money off your trolley load at the till.

◆ Hold one of those 'Virgin Vie' or 'Body Shop' style parties at home. Get your friends round to spend their money, then as the host you'll *usually get a free gift or a voucher for products, so stock up on gifts for free. Check the Internet for company head office contact numbers.*

◆ *There are lots of 'freebie' websites out there where you can register for free samples. See the MoneySavingExpert.com freebies board, then save the freebies and use as presents.*

◆ *Funky bookmarks can be easily made from a length of very narrow ribbon or some embroidery thread. Knot one end and thread on a few glass or plastic beads (like those found in little girls' jewellery kits or picked up at craft shops), knot again to hold in place, leave about 10 inches of ribbon or thread and repeat the process at the other end with matching beads. Works like a bookmark with the pretty beads hanging out of the top and bottom of the book. Perfect for grannies, aunties, teachers, friends and anyone who enjoys reading. Costs pennies and looks great.*

◆ *Most people have got stacks of photos sitting around that they've never got around to sticking in albums so make up an album with some of the year's highlights in; you can buy flip-over albums quite cheaply in pound shops, Wilkinsons and supermarkets.*

◆ *If you're computer literate, print out some personalised stationery. You can be as creative as you like and it saves a fortune on having the stuff printed professionally. Buy some cheap boxes and put it in with envelopes all wrapped up with ribbon.*

Seasonal Presents

Easter Gifts

If you want to give Easter eggs buy some of those chocolate moulds and make your own using cooking chocolate, which you can buy in the supermarket.

> # REAL OLD-STYLE STORY
>
> Inspired by a visit to the local market, I'm not going to get my kids Easter eggs. I'm going to the stall where you can get stuff like 10 Aeros for £1 and five big bags of jelly sweets for £1, getting a little selection of stuff and making them Easter boxes and baskets. I'm going to make mini nests using the paper from my shredder. We're also going to decorate eggs; you can make a lovely marbled effect by boiling them in water with onion skins. The natural colour in the onion skins dyes the eggs. And my mum used to scrunch up a couple of Shredded Wheat and mix with a melted Mars Bar to make 'nests' she would then fill with mini-eggs.

Father's Day Gifts

Gift vouchers for services are cheap but much appreciated. Think of something that your dad really hates doing and mock up a voucher for it, such as mowing the grass, washing the car, cleaning out the junk cupboard, painting the shed or whatever. Alternatively, you can do vouchers like 'good for one cake of your choice to be baked by yours truly' or 'good for one picnic'. For more ideas check out www.fun-vouchers.org.uk

REAL OLD-STYLE STORY

I got organised last week with my kids and we did handprints in clay which make fantastic presents and lovely keepsakes, especially for grandparents. It was a fun couple of hours after tea that the kids enjoyed... being let loose in my craft drawers is like sheer heaven to them. Mind you, clearing up afterwards is not so enjoyable!

Anniversary Gifts

◆ One fun idea is to set a really low budget for how much you're going to spend, say £5 each, then find five things that remind you of something about the person or of your time together. Rummage through the charity or pound shops.

◆ Or make anniversary stockings as you would at Christmas for the kids and put in small budget-priced prezzies rather than splashing out on something expensive.

◆ Home-cooked meals with candles can beat a meal out in a posh restaurant, and you can always pretend you've gone out by leaving the washing up! Or give one of your kids some extra pocket money to do it for you.

◆ A home-made book with 'promises' for foot massages, home-cooked meals and the like...

REAL OLD-STYLE STORY

The day before our anniversary we had a lovely bath. Hubby made me an appointment at the hairdressers and then took me out for a meal in a hotel using the voucher his boss had given him for Christmas last year. It meant he had to pay 65p for the night out. We went home, watched some telly we both wanted to see and fell asleep in each other's arms!

School Fêtes and Raffles

◆ Last-minute request from the cake stall at school? Keep a couple of cheapie 'value' or budget cakes in the cupboard that you can ice and pass off as your own.

◆ Grocery hampers can easily be made up including home-made bread, biscuits or jams.

◆ Pressure to find gifts for the tombola? Remember that gift cupboard? Also a chance to get rid of any unused toiletries you've been given for Christmas or birthdays.

◆ Take some cuttings along – there's often a plant stall at local fêtes and fairs.

WRAPPING UP

Okay, you've made it, bought it in the sale or just had it kicking around at home, now it's time to wrap up all those goodies but true Old-Stylers won't waste loads of money on expensive gift wrap and packaging.

◆ Keep a shelf in your gift cupboard for any spare packaging like bubble wrap, Jiffy bags, boxes and the like. Most gift bags can be reused if you just cut off the tag.

◆ Cheap wicker baskets make good containers for an assortment of food gifts. You can line them with paper napkins put at different angles to each other and overlapping the sides.

◆ Look for rolls of plain coloured paper in the sales. Jazz it up with ribbons and bows and it looks good for either birthday or Christmas presents.

◆ To make your own bows, get a rectangular piece of matching gift wrap, cut a fringe all the way along and then, using the scissors at an angle of each piece of fringe, scrape them along it, giving it a curled effect. When it's all done, fold the base up concertina fashion and stick to the present with double-sided tape. Arrange the fronds of the bow so you can't see the plain side.

◆ To make funky but cheap wrapping paper, get a roll of wall lining paper (often less than £2 a roll), water down some emulsion and, using kitchen roll, paint, 'rag' or 'sponge' it to make marbled wrapping paper.

◆ Get the kids to stamp designs on brown paper using shapes cut from cheap bathroom sponges or potatoes.

◆ Wrap presents in brown paper and stencil flowers or designs on it; kids will love this and they can colour them in.

◆ It's also worth checking DIY stores for end-of-roll bits of wallpaper that can be used as wrapping paper.

◆ Keep all the gift tags, bows and paper you can. It saves spending a fortune in the shops; especially with kids it's ripped off in seconds so they'll never notice if it's not ironing board flat to start with.

◆ Keep used tissue paper to wrap clothes or shoes.

◆ For fancy cellophane ask your local florist who can sell it off the roll to you; cheaper than buying in card shops.

◆ Find a gorgeous piece of material; scan it on the computer and print it out in colour to use as wrapping paper. It's best if you've got a printer that can cope with A3 paper, or photocopy the material if you can get away with using the work photocopier; even the local library may have an A3 copier.

Gift Tags

◆   *These can be designed and printed on the computer; then, like the*
    trendy shops, attach them with old fashioned string or a safety pin
    and say you bought them from a 'quaint little home-made place'.

◆   *Cut down old birthday, Easter and Christmas cards with pinking*
    shears for cheap tags.

◆   *Print a wallet-sized picture of the recipient for their gift tag.*

Professional Wrapping the Old-Style Way

In the posh shops they wrap gifts for you (usually at a price!) so watch
any in-store demonstrations (especially near Christmas) to learn the
tricks of the trade.

Try getting some coloured tissue paper – a couple of sheets in
contrasting colours is ideal – and wrap the present, scrunching the
ends at the top. Then put a piece of fine net over the top, gather the
ends of the tissue paper and put matching or contrasting ribbons
around it. You can contrast the colours as the tissue shows through
the net. Looks expensive!

You can buy net material cheaply if you look in the remnant box
in department stores. Shiny polyester material (like satin) wrapped
around a present and tied at the top with ribbons looks good too; cut
the edges with pinking shears or zigzag scissors.

REAL OLD-STYLE STORY

My daughter forgot to get gift wrap for a birthday present for her boyfriend's mum. She was due to give the present at a party that evening. As the shops had all shut, this was an emergency of the highest order. So I found a red paper tablecloth – there was a pile in the garage left over from some do I'd catered for – and a roll of cellophane like you get on flowers or gift baskets (that came from a flower market). We wrapped the present in the red tablecloth, added lots of flower petals picked from the balcony, next the cellophane and then a toning ribbon. The petals were just what was available at the time. If it's winter you could try ivy leaves. The boyfriend's mum thought it had been professionally gift-wrapped.

Children's Gifts

It's that classic case of spending a fortune on the kids' presents and then they spend more time playing with the boxes they came in. What's 'in' today with kids' toys is forgotten tomorrow and it's usually 'quantity' they're after rather than 'quality'. Given the choice, most children would rather have a whole heap of presents to open than just one more-expensive present.

Think of a theme – such as the hobby they're into, like art – and make an 'art kit'; back to the hamper idea. Get a little wicker basket in a charity shop and fill it with pens and pencils and paint brushes, ruler, rubber and a sharpener.

Or go for a 'foodie' kit for kids – apron, rolling pin, gingerbread cutters, an easy recipe and little bags of ingredients. And don't forget the toppings like hundreds and thousands.

For girls you can make an entire wardrobe of clothes for their favourite doll. Offcuts of material or remnants from your sewing basket are ideal and they'll have instant designer wear. Copy one of the child's favourite outfits and make a smaller size for their doll. Or make them a rag doll; you can find patterns online – try www.ragdollroom.com for free downloads of patterns for both dolls and their clothes.

And relive your *Blue Peter* days by making rooms, houses and scenes for dolls, trains or dumper trucks. Use your imagination and make a farmyard from a piece of hardboard painted green with rivers and roads or make army scenes, hairdressing salons or petrol stations. Much cheaper than those plastic sets sold in toy stores and not a huge waste of money if they're into something else by next year.

A selection of coloured modelling stuff along with cheap cookie cutters will do for little ones. Here's an easy recipe for making your own play dough:

Play Dough

1 cup plain flour
½ cup salt
2 tbsp cream of tartar
225ml (8fl oz) water with food colouring added

Place all ingredients in a large saucepan over a steady heat. Stir until it forms into a ball. Allow to cool. Knead until smooth and store in a zip-lock bag. You can make up small bags or pots for party bags. When it starts to go hard, add 1 tbsp oil, warm in the microwave and it's nice and soft again.

CHILDREN'S PARTIES

Where once a few games of pass the parcel and a bowl of jelly and ice cream would have kept them entertained, kids' parties are now big business with the average party spend around £150. Instead of paying for organised party companies to come to your house and host the party for you, organise your own – just rope in a few other parents to help you.

Craft Parties

There are loads of those pottery-style cafés around where you can paint
your own mugs and animal ceramics but they can cost around £15 per
person for a session. Buy up some plain china (car boot sales are
ideal), dig out some paints and let little and bigger ones design their
own mugs, cups and plates.

Charlie and the Chocolate Factory Party

Send out 'Golden Tickets' wrapped around small bars of chocolate,
copying the wording from the book/film. When the children arrive, get
them making chocolates or an easy chocolate recipe like chocolate Rice
Krispie cakes. Okay, so there's a bit of clearing up to do, and it
probably only works if you have a decent-sized kitchen, but fun for the
kids. After tea they can watch the film (borrow a copy from the library if
you haven't got one).

Girlie Pamper Parties

Girls of around eight will love the chance to play make-up and dressing
up. Get a load of old make-up – lipsticks, nail varnishes, that kind of
thing – and put them into baskets. When they arrive serve 'cocktails' in
plastic champagne flutes (lemonade with a few drops of food colouring
goes down a treat in blue, pink or their favourite colour) and make the

centre of the room into a cosy bedsit with quilts, cushions and beanbags. Get a friend to help and give them a mini pedicure or manicure, then they can have home-made popcorn while watching a movie. For party bags, buy up some packs of mini lip gloss or nail varnish, wrap in clear cellophane bags with coloured confetti, secured with funky hair bobbles.

Chapter 7

CHRISTMAS, WEDDINGS AND OTHER OCCASIONS

You don't have to be Scrooge to know that Christmas has become hideously over-commercialised. In recent years fights have broken out as parents struggle to get their children the latest 'must have' toy, and there seems no end to the list of presents you can buy – for everyone from your child's teacher to the neighbours, your postman, milkman . . . You can quite literally go on forever!

This chapter's about re-creating an Old-Style festive season with home-made gifts, cards, wrapping and hampers.

And when it comes to celebrations, weddings must rank as probably the single most expensive day of your life (after signing up for a mortgage) so in what ways can you cut back without spoiling your day?

THE COMPLETE OLD-STYLE CHRISTMAS STARTS HERE . . .

Instead of buying for everyone you've ever met, cut down to immediate family and a few close friends. If you're caught up in one of those 'we'd better get something in case they buy us something' circles, agree upfront not to buy or maybe to set a price limit of, say, £5 to get each other a box of biscuits or chocolates, or better still go Old-Style and make your own.

Children love giving and receiving presents, and would happily let you buy for the whole class, so try and agree to do a 'Secret Santa' with the other parents or teachers where each child takes in one present which can be put into a box and given out anonymously. This works just as well in the office when there's that dilemma of whether you buy for the boss and end up looking a creep or look a tightwad if everyone else does and you don't.

Be organised: draw up a present list and stick to it. Carry it round with you so whenever you spot a bargain or make something, you can tick off the person's name.

Christmas Budgeting

To avoid getting into debt come January (and let's face it, it's no great surprise that Christmas happens each and every year on 25th December) start saving in January, paying in something like £20 a month. Even £20 a month turns into £240 in a year plus interest. For

full details on the very best way to get maximum interest, see
www.moneysavingexpert.com/christmassaving

Spread the Cost

◆   Chip in with brothers and sisters to buy for parents or other relatives
     rather than all buying individual presents.

◆   Save up all your Tesco Reward vouchers, Nectar or Boots points, and
     anywhere else you earn loyalty points that can be used for money off,
     and cash them in on the final Christmas shop.

◆   At least two months before Christmas make a list of all the food you
     usually buy and find those with the longest shelf life. Buy a couple of
     things each week with the usual weekly food shop to save a huge bill
     at the end.

◆   If you've got lots of presents to buy and haven't got around to
     starting your 'gift cupboard', make it a rule to buy a couple of
     presents each week to ease the cost and hassle. Same goes for
     everything else: buying a pack of stamps a week and even writing a
     couple of cards a week gets the job done easier than in one go.

◆   Being organised and buying early is great, but when it comes to kids
     and the fact they change their mind at the last minute you are often
     better off saving the 'big' presents till the last minute in the hope of
     snaffling a bargain in the pre-Christmas sales.

◆   Go on holiday! Yep, it's often cheaper to book a week or so in the sun
     than shell out on all the food, presents, cards, trimmings, panto,
     works party and so on.

Cards and Gift Wrap

Cards

Agree with family and friends not to send cards but make a donation to a charity instead. Send e-cards – cheaper than the real thing and saves wrecking your nails opening all those envelopes. If you're handy with a needle, cross-stitch cards – they can be framed and kept forever. Get the kids to design and make their own by cutting, sticking and making potato prints, or take a family snap and print it off on home-made cards. Cards with the kids' hand prints on are great for little ones who can't write or draw – one Old-Styler made reindeer for the front of her Christmas cards and used her daughter's hand print as the antlers. See also page 154 for more details on card-making.

Santa Letters

The latest thing now for kids is to get a reply from Santa once they've written him a letter. There are lots of websites where you can order personalised fancy 'Santa' replies at around £5 a go, but for a freebie send your letter to Santa Claus, Reindeerland, SAN TA1 and your child will get a reply. Check the Royal Mail's website (www.royalmail.com) for the last date for replies, which is usually mid-December. And some supermarkets have post boxes in store in which you can post your letters to get a reply from Santa.

Wrapping

◆ Buy up gift tags, cards and rolls of wrapping in the sales, or go creative and make your own. The kids can do hand prints or potato stamps on brown paper or just draw pictures on it.

◆ Keep a box throughout the year with wrapping paper, ribbons, tissue paper, Jiffy bags and the like as it's not just the 'pretty' wrapping that costs a fortune; the outer layer to get it through the post safely costs too.

◆ Florists sell flower cellophane really cheaply and it's great for wrapping home-made hampers, baskets and home-grown pots.

◆ Plain brown paper, tied with twine and fastened with a sprig of mistletoe or ivy looks simple but effective and has a slightly old-fashioned Christmas appeal to it.

Gift Tags

◆ Reuse old Christmas cards cut into wacky shapes with pinking shears.

◆ Use photos or pictures from magazines.

◆ At www.graphicgarden.com they have loads of free printable labels and tags you can use.

Gifts

There are lots of present ideas in Chapter 6, and the voucher one is always good for Christmas. Make your own with an offer of Saturday night babysitting, a 'girlie shopping trip' with coffee and cake included or a massage, pedicure, promise of mowing the lawn, cleaning the

kitchen, doing the chores for a weekend or making a picnic. Try
www.fun-vouchers.org.uk to create your own.

Gift Ideas

◆ *Look out for the '3 for 2' BOGOF deals at Christmas in places like
Woolies and M&S. Great for stocking fillers or presents for children's
friends, and handy for a standby when you suddenly need an
'emergency' present.*

◆ *Make your own Christmas hamper with fresh produce from your local
farm shop. It's cheaper than buying ready-made and you can choose
what goes in it (see 'Home-made Hampers', on page 184).*

◆ *Or make home-made shortbread, jams, pickles or chocolates and
parcel them up in pretty boxes tied with ribbon.*

◆ *Make mini-Christmas puds in washed-out and lined baked bean tins.
When they're done, tie them round with some thick Christmas ribbon
(saved from prezzies you had last Christmas).*

◆ *Buy a pot or tub for the garden, fill with compost and plant bulbs,
cover with cling film and tie a ribbon round it. When the bulbs come
out in spring they will get a lovely surprise!*

◆ *Cushions – a good way to use up scraps of material and dead easy to
make. Literally two squares sewn together and stuffed.*

◆ *Lavender bags are also really quick and easy to make but need to be
done a bit nearer Christmas so the smell doesn't fade.*

◆ *A beautifully bound collection of poems or recipes all typed up and
made into a nice book.*

Creative Gifts

◆   Get the kids to be creative by mixing up a paste of flour and water;
     you can make all sorts of things like coasters, bowls and pots. Bake in
     the oven on a hot temperature till they're set and then paint.

◆   Buy up some cheap white candles (IKEA sells them) and some
     modelling clay and make candle holders in the shape of stars, holly
     leaves, the moon...

◆   Make calendars with anything from drawings the children have done
     to a lovely family photo. The 'date' part can be bought quite cheaply
     in shops like Clintons, Woolies or Smiths.

◆   Make trendy coasters from old CDs or singles. Use your own or buy
     up cheaply at charity shops.

◆   Get some plain white mugs and put the kids' hand prints on them;
     you'll need special ceramic paints so ask in an art and craft shop to
     get the right sort.

Presents for Children

◆   'Grow your own' kits with a flower pot, small bag of compost and
     seeds are great for little green fingers.

◆   Handy with a sewing machine? What about home-made dressing-up
     outfits or hand puppets, or T-shirts decorated with fabric paints with
     names and designs on?

◆   For dolls' houses and forts there's a bit of DIY effort involved unless you
     can do it Blue Peter style with cardboard boxes and sticky-back plastic.

◆   Clothes for kids are a good idea, especially if you don't know what
     toys they've got. Asda, Tesco and Sainsbury's all do great value kids'
     stuff – cheap and cheerful T-shirts, tops, hats and bags.

◆ *Avoid giving gift vouchers as these can't be bought in the sales, everyone knows how much you've spent, and chances are you'll 'round up' to a tenner the amount you were going to spend. Buy a prezzie instead.*

◆ *Check out charity shops like Oxfam that often sell locally crafted pieces from around the world.*

Home-made Hampers

◆ *Home-made jams and chutneys make great presents. Stick some pretty labels or tags on.*

◆ *Or home-made chocolates or petits fours wrapped in tissue paper in a pretty box.*

◆ *Or home-made Old-Style shortbread. It's cheap, easy to make – even with the kids – and tastes good! See the recipe opposite.*

◆ *Themed food hampers can be made for anyone – for someone who loves Italian food pack the hamper with pesto sauce, garlic, oils, dried pasta, tomato sauces and so on. Or do a 'cheese' hamper with lots of speciality cheeses, some beer and posh crackers.*

◆ *No need to stick to 'food' hampers; make a 'relax' hamper with bath goodies. Buying in bulk means packs of soap, flannels and bath bombs can be split, saving money. Or do the hamper in a particular colour theme.*

◆ *For the 'hamper' buy wicker baskets in garden centres or at the pound shop.*

Home-made Old-Style Shortbread

170g (6oz) plain flour
115g (4oz) butter
55g (2oz) caster sugar, plus some to sprinkle

Put all the ingredients in a bowl, mix well by hand until the mixture is like a crumble. Keep going and it'll stick together. Roll out, cut out shapes, bake in a medium oven for 15–20 minutes. It's also good dipped in melted chocolate for a more luxurious type.

Decorations

◆ *Make a Christmas candle wreath Blue Peter style – get an old wire coat hanger, bend it into a circle and attach tinsel and candles.*

◆ *Check out school Christmas fairs for cheap decorations.*

◆ *Make some of those old-fashioned paper chains with strips of gummed paper; they sell them in places like Hawkins Bazaar. Or make them from strips of coloured paper and glue each one into a circle shape before attaching the next.*

◆ *Remember, 'less is more' – go for the minimalist look with Christmas decorations. Simple and tasteful is better than buying tons of stuff that doesn't go and just looks gaudy and tacky.*

Home-made Christmas Crackers

Hang on to all those mottos, toys and gifts from crackers (they always end up in the bin just after lunch) and make your own crackers with the innards of toilet rolls and some pretty crêpe paper.

Or buy really basic, cheap crackers in the January sales and embellish them by sticking in some extra gifts saved from last year's crackers or home-made.

Food and Drink

Old-Style Christmas Nibbles (saves pounds in your pocket and on your waistline!)
These can of course be made any time of year, and making your own saves buying all those packets of party nibbles that look great on the outside but are stodgy and disappointing when they come out of the oven at Christmas. Some ideas are:

- *Deep-fried potato skins.*
- *Bread sticks dipped in olive oil, wrapped in a couple of basil leaves and a slice of Parma ham, cold meat or cheese.*
- *For 'nuts' without the calories drain a can of chickpeas, stick them on a tray in the oven till hot and serve.*
- *For low-fat crisps, cook up some sheets of lasagne, and when soft cut them into small shapes and triangles, place on a baking tray with a squirt of olive oil and bake.*

Christmas Booze

Buy a bottle of the cheapest vodka you can find and flavour it with sweets or fruit. Werther's Original toffees can be added for toffee flavour or you could use extra-strong mints, chocolate or pear drops. Liquorice is good too but takes ages to dissolve. Or try vodka with a vanilla pod added.

Using Up the Leftover Turkey

◆ *Boil up the carcass for soup.*

◆ *Use the 'bits' for curries, coronation chicken, enchiladas or tacos, or add flour and breadcrumbs to turn them into home-made nuggets.*

◆ *The wings can be smothered in barbecue sauce (home-made or bought) and served with rice or spicy wedges.*

◆ *Make turkey and veggie pie.*

◆ *Stir-fry with some of the leftover vegetables.*

◆ *Make sandwiches for Christmas Day tea.*

Using Up the Leftover Veg

◆ *Make bubble and squeak to have with cold turkey.*

◆ *Mix with an egg and some flour to bind, form into rounds and roast in the oven for about 20 minutes until cooked.*

◆ *Make vegetable soup – cook up with some veggie stock, add some milk or cream and whiz through in a food processor. You could combine this with the leftover turkey.*

◆ *Feed it to someone else – mix it in with the dog's food!*

- *Make a 'hash' by cooking up all the veg, adding the meat, Yorkshire puds, anything that's left and pile a load of gravy on top!*
- *Blitz any leftovers in the food processor and use as stuffing for boned chicken.*

MONEYSAVING WEDDINGS

They say it's the biggest day of your life, and financially at least that's always true. The ultimate romantic gesture isn't far from being the biggest single cost around, and its impact permeates through families. Judging by the surveys from some of the bridal magazines, that one day can cost around £20,000, so let's try to cut that cost.

Much wedding MoneySaving is a question of compromise and prioritisation. While a wedding is a wonderful dream day, if it leaves you financially crippled and paying it off for most of your married years, it's a pointless waste. Therefore the first step is to plan how much cash you are willing and able to spend, where it is going to come from, and what you are going to spend it on.

The truth is the cost of getting married will always swell to fill the budget. You never hear 'what are we going to do with the extra cash?' So sit down and plan through what cash you have to spend, who's going to pay and where it comes from.

Prioritising

The idea is to have a wonderful day but for the best value. Much of this involves priorities. It's worth balancing out the value of different things.

Which is more important to you: a professional photographer, great flowers on the table or beautifully hand-crafted invitations? Weigh up your priorities.

Ms Thrift Got Married

In the early days of MoneySavingExpert.com one of the regulars in the Chat Forum, Ms Thrift (now Mrs Thrift), started a discussion about how to cut the cost of a wedding.

This became hugely popular and the discussion still rages on, with lots of really invaluable new suggestions. There are many ways to cut the costs of weddings. The best thing to do is spend time reading through people's original suggestions which can be found at www.moneysavingexpert.com/weddings, and of course you can add your own thoughts. Here are just some of the suggestions.

The Big One: Involve Friends and Family

One of the main themes running through the discussion is to make sure you use your friends' and families' core skills. Many people you know will be able to help so instead of simply setting down a wedding list, have a think through who can do what and ask them personally – it's a much nicer gift.

So do you know a cake-maker or a decent photographer? Is your brother a DJ or musician? Do you have an aunt or uncle with a landscaped garden they'll let you use for the reception? Or is a relative in the printing trade?

Stationery

◆ *Print your own. Whatever you want it is possible to print it – invitations, orders of service, menus, place names and thank-you cards. All the things you'll need for DIY printing are available for free on the Internet at sites like Wedding Crafter and Mad about Cards.*

◆ *Will work help? See if your work will let you use their company discount on stationery.*

◆ *A picture says a thousand thank-yous. Find a really good photo of the two of you, have the negative reprinted as many times as necessary and handwrite on the back of it your personal thank-yous.*

Making the Blushing Bride Even More Beautiful

Think out of the Box

Buy your wedding dress off the rail in department stores such as Debenhams rather than having it made to order. Oxfam even have wedding outlets. Asda now has its own range of budget-priced dresses from £60 in many of its larger stores.

Handy Second-hand Items

Why buy brand-new items that are going to be used once then spend the rest of their days dust-gathering in the attic? Try using eBay or other second-hand retailers for things like veils or bridesmaids' tiaras. Alternatively, replace these items with much cheaper substitutes like flowers in your hair.

Use Credit Loopholes

Some stores, such as Debenhams, have store cards offering an initial 10 per cent discount when opened. If you don't have any debt problems take advantage of these by applying for a card and using the discount when buying your dress. Just make sure you pay it off in full at the end of the month or you'll be charged a ton of interest. See www.moneysavingexpert.com/storecards for more details.

Make Friends in Selfridges

Get your make-up done in a large cosmetics department, somewhere like the Estée Lauder counter, on your special day, then simply buy the lipstick to 'touch up' (and why not ask if they'll give you that as a freebie sample?)

Photography

Hijack Friends' Footage

Many of your guests will record the day for posterity, so why not ask them for a copy of their photos and videos? You can encourage this further by leaving cheap disposable cameras on the tables at the reception and collecting them in at the end of the night.

Ask at Local Colleges
Students on photography courses might be glad of the experience and the chance to add to their portfolio in return for a small fee. If you're prepared to let them use your snaps online you may also be able to agree a better rate or even persuade them not to bill you for their time but just any snaps you buy.

Venues

Be Different
Pick an unpopular day for the wedding. Having it on a Thursday, Friday or Sunday can reduce the cost of the reception (and sometimes ceremony) venue by up to half. Generally, any non-Saturday booking will receive some discount.

Reception

Use the Personal Touch
Styling the reception yourself can be time-consuming but much, much cheaper. Inexpensive alternatives can then be used instead of common costly items, such as white bed sheets as tablecloths. If you have friends with spare time, why not ask them to help as a wedding present to you?

Booze Cruise

This one's a near-must for anyone doing the reception themselves. Taking a quick (and low-cost) day trip to France/Belgium will allow you to pick up plenty of crates of cheap booze and champagne. The saving should more than outweigh the travel cost (though it's always worth checking this by pricing your booze list in the UK first and then using the Internet to price it overseas).

Free Glass Hire

You can further decrease your costs by arranging free glass hire (Waitrose and Morrisons currently offer this).

Do Me a Favour

Making your own favours for the guests can be a lot more personal and much cheaper. There are loads of possibilities for this, even printing out fancy envelopes and filling them with lottery tickets.

Let Others Do the Worrying, Cheaply

Delay booking the Master of Ceremonies until the last minute. Then, if they want the job, they'll still do it and this can halve the price. Better still, ask a confident friend to do it for you. Further down the food chain, trainee cooks and waiters can sometimes be hired cheaply from colleges.

Wedding Presents

Weddings are a great chance to get some presents, and by doing a list you (hopefully) avoid getting five kettles, 10 toasters and 30 vases. Of course you can do this the old-fashioned way and trawl stores for the things you like, write them in a notebook and get everyone to ring up your folks or whoever is co-ordinating the list to check what's on it before they buy. Or you can get one of the department stores like John Lewis, Next, Debenhams or Argos to have the list for you. Check out those that offer incentives – Debenhams gives you a £50 voucher when you register your list with them, the loophole being that your guests don't even have to buy anything from it; so you can have a list with, say, Next but register with Debenhams to get your free £50.

Instead of having 'presents' on the wedding list, you could ask people if they'd be prepared to chip in and cover the cost of the cake, wedding photos, flowers and so on as their gift.

Honeymoon

It may sound obvious but shop around for your honeymoon. If you're flexible on destination and brave enough to wait you can cut the cost even further.

Always make sure you check out free upgrades and specials for honeymooners, and speak directly with the travel company. It's also worth letting an airline know you're on honeymoon. There's a tiny chance you may just get an upgrade.

Holiday or a Toaster?

You could have a honeymoon fund instead of a wedding present list. People are waiting longer before marrying nowadays and often already have a home and the main household gadgets when they get married, so why not ask friends and families to make contributions towards the honeymoon instead?

Cake

Home Decorating

Buy a simple sponge cake, or whatever takes your fancy, from the supermarket and then decorate it yourself. Marks & Spencer do a range of wedding cakes (all different-sized tiers) for a fraction of the cost of having one made.

Size isn't Everything

To avoid massive cost and waste, make individual wedding cup cakes for each of your guests.

The Ring

Use smaller shops and try to avoid big retailers. Websites like www.goldfinger-rings.com can also be very reasonable.

Flowers

Innovate
It's amazing what you can do with some cheap vases, spray paints and a bit of elbow grease.

Don't Overlook Little Shops
Good quality flowers can be found cheaply at the village market or down the local grocer's shop.

Give to Charity
The British Heart Foundation sells fake roses for £1, brilliant for button holes. As well as contributing to a good cause, they don't die or get crushed by all the hugging.

Transport

Look the Part, for Less
Those who don't live in London can go for a London-style cab as a wedding car and you'll get the smart black transport type of atmosphere at a much lower cost.

Don't Drive
If you are having a civil wedding, by using the same venue for all parts of the day, no transport will be needed.

Miscellaneous

Say it with Soap

Use bubbles instead of expensive confetti! Or make the confetti yourself by cutting up sheets of wrapping paper.

Use Martin's MoneySaving Mantras

Stick to your budget. Whatever you're buying always ask 'will we use it, is it worth it, can we find it cheaper anywhere else?'

BIRTHDAYS

They come round every year but it's always harder to think of different ideas, particularly for children. There are lots of ideas for children's parties in Chapter 6 but here are some more foodie ones.

◆ *For birthday tea, basic foods like burgers and chips are always popular – vary the burgers by, say, adding a slice of pineapple for a Hawaiian burger, bacon for Danish, garlic added to the mince and topped with Brie for Parisian and so on. Hot dogs in rolls (with or without onion) are another good idea.*

◆ *Dig out the fondue set and make a great chocolate one with marshmallows, strawberries, kiwi fruit and banana slices to dip in it.*

◆ *Buffet-style spreads can be difficult. It's hard to work out just how much people will eat so you have enough but without tons being left over. Sandwiches with the crusts cut off and cut into bite-sized pieces are cheap and easy to make; sausages on sticks, quiches, a rice salad* with spring onions, and brightly coloured veggies like peppers go a long way. Fresh bread and a cheese board or pâté means those with a bigger appetite can go back and 'pick'.

REAL OLD-STYLE STORY

Every year when I was growing up it was either a birthday tea party with family and a few friends or my favourite tea of all time... mix and match. Basically a whole loaf of bread was put on the table with every conceivable filling or spread that was in the house. We all got to make up our own sarnies and could mix and match whatever we wanted. The only rule was, if you made it you had to eat it. Some weird combinations used to get passed around I can tell you — Marmite and pickle, corned beef and fish paste. It was great fun.

Novelty Birthday Cakes

Buy them in the shops and they'll cost around £8 plus but with a few budget-priced sponges and a bit of creativity you can create your own.

Football Pitch

Cover a rectangular sponge cake in butter icing. Stick chocolate fingers round the sides to make a fence. Put some desiccated coconut in a Tupperware box with a few drops of green food colouring and shake hard. Cover the top of the cake with the green coconut.

Pipe on pitch markings with white icing. Make goals with bamboo skewers bent into shape, and corner flags with pieces of skewer or cocktail sticks, with gummed paper flags on.

Tardis

Bake a cake in a loaf tin. Stand on end and cover in blue roll-out icing. Pipe on features and add a blue gobstopper-type sweet on the top for the light.

Hedgehog

Bake a sponge in a pudding basin then cover in chocolate butter icing. Use chocolate flakes to make the spines and add marzipan feet and eyes.

Cat's Face

Get a standard round sponge and shape out two ears at the top. Cover in butter icing then decorate with sweets for eyes, nose and whiskers.

Fairy Castle

Great for using up bits and pieces of cake from the cupboard. Put various shapes of cake on a base. Cover in ready-rolled white icing. Add a tower or two and various sugar decorations such as flowers, silver balls and sweets. Use marshmallows for the steps up to the castle door.

Teddy Bears' Tea Party

Get a round sponge sandwich cake and cover with a roll-out icing 'tablecloth'. Make stools for the bears to sit on in the same way with mini fairy cakes, then make plates out of circles of roll-out icing. Food can be made from cake offcuts (from making the chairs and table flat!) and also little sweets like dolly mixtures and liquorice allsorts. Those square sandwich-type sweets can be cut into triangles to look like little sandwiches.

HAVING A BABY

The huge cost of feeding, clothing and educating a child could well be enough to put anyone off having kids in the first place. It's reckoned to cost around £150,000 to bring a child up to age 21 – though that includes pretty much every last thing you'd ever need plus university education – but it's a sobering thought so here's how to bring up baby the Old-Style way.

What You Don't Need

◆ *Changing mat – don't bother with it; use a towel on the floor.*

◆ *Expensive baby wipes – use cotton wool and warm water or flannels that can be boil washed or stuck in the machine after wiping mucky faces.*

◆ *Formula milk – breast-feeding is cheaper and meant to be better for the baby. If you do use formula, shop around – it's often cheaper at* the baby clinic than in the supermarket.

◆ Tinned baby food – just make your own purées and freeze in ice cube trays before defrosting in the morning.

◆ New prams and equipment – look for second-hand items; this can save hundreds of pounds. Try eBay, boot fairs and second-hand shops. When they're small they're not in them long enough to justify spending a fortune.

◆ Expensive clothes – they often get messed up and are constantly in the wash so a cheap and cheerful backup supply is great. If friends and family want to buy baby clothes, ask for sizes for three or six months plus – anyone having a baby gets so much stuff for 'newborn' they won't get around to wearing most of it before they grow, so this way you'll have a year's worth of clothes already. Primark and Peacocks are good for basic and cheap baby clothes, and babygro outfits and vests can be found for around 5–10p at boot fairs and jumble sales.

◆ Expensive wallpaper in the nursery – they'll soon grow out of it so paint the walls in a plain colour and buy those character 'stickarounds' from places like Homebase and B&Q that peel off. This way you can give the room a mini-makeover really easily. Just put up a new pair of curtains and quilt cover (bought from eBay) in their latest craze, whether it's Barbie, Superman or whatever, and you've got a whole new room. Make sure you sell the covers/curtains back again yourself afterwards.

◆ New stair gates, fireguards and travel cots – all good bargains at boot fairs and on eBay.

◆ New toys and books – join a local toy library and borrow books from your local library.

Other MoneySaving Tips

◆ *Stock up on BOGOFs. If you're using disposable nappies wait till there's a deal on and buy them up, though reusable do work out cheaper. Don't think they just look like pieces of cloth either; they are similar to disposable nappies but with a washable inner lining. See www.moneysavingexpert.com/nappies*

◆ *IKEA is really rated for kids' bedroom furniture, and even the basics like plastic plates, knives, forks and spoons for when they get older. There are some great traditional 'wooden' toys in there for a few pounds, and large chunky plastic storage crates for their toys.*

◆ *Save on huge childcare bills by organising a childcare share with other parents, so everyone gets to have one or two days' childcare a week.*

◆ *Have a baby list like a wedding list. If people are going to buy presents, it's far better to have ones that fulfil your needs.*

◆ *Hang on to any vouchers you get. Mother and baby clubs often give them out. Pick up your free 'bounty' pack from the doctor or hospital – there are often loads of vouchers/samples in there too.*

◆ *Join every 'baby club' going – Boots, Tesco, Mothercare – as soon as you're pregnant. Ask in local stores for details or check their websites – there are loads of freebies and vouchers on offer.*

CHRISTENINGS/BABY CELEBRATIONS

Presents

◆ A good gift for christenings is a bible. It costs around £5 from places like M&S and Usborne Books.

◆ The 'mug, bowl, plate' packages in bone china with Winnie the Pooh or Beatrix Potter characters can be quite pricey in the shops but are much cheaper from factory outlets.

◆ Practical presents are often welcome so what about getting a big fluffy bath towel with the child's name embroidered on it?

◆ Get a decent bottle of wine and attach a label saying it's to be opened on the child's 18th, 21st or wedding.

◆ Children's classics like Wind in the Willows and Winnie the Pooh can often be picked up in those discounted bookshops at half price and they look really expensive, often selling new for £20–£25.

◆ Buy a newspaper on the day of the christening (or, even better, the day of the birth) and box it up as a gift; if you buy it on the day you'll get a present for less than £1.

Food

Keep the cost down by doing a buffet at home. Either enlist the help of family and friends to bring along a dish or head down to Iceland or Asda and stock up on their frozen 'nibble' selection. A really good cheeseboard, fresh bread and crackers and grapes and fruit will give any shop-bought buffet a more home-prepared look.

For cheap drink for those in the southeast of England, take a day trip to France to stock up and look out for any special deals on bubbly – sites like www.fixtureferrets.co.uk are good for checking out special offer prices. Buying own-brand champagne or Cava is loads cheaper than your 'Bolly' or Moët and most people will never tell the difference. Or add some orange juice to sparkling wine and serve a Bucks Fizz when guests arrive.

Cakes

Either make one or buy from a place like Costco that sells large cakes (approximately 20 x 12 inches) all iced for around £10.

For more great MoneySaving ideas go to the Old-Style thread at www.moneysavingexpert.com/oschristenings

Chapter 8

THE OLD-STYLE RECIPE BOOK

A lot of cookery books call for fancy ingredients and a whole load of mucking about in the kitchen. But Old-Style cookery is about looking at what's in the cupboard and what you can make with it. You don't need to rush out to buy more ingredients that are likely to sit half-used at the back of your cupboard well beyond their 'best before' date.

Obviously it's impossible to include all the Old-Style recipes in this Old-Style cookery book, it's just a selection. Take your pick from soups and main courses, veggie dishes, late-night pub grub and snacks or ideas for packed lunches. And you can find out the everyday essential ingredients for any well-stocked store cupboard, as well as some of the kitchen appliances worth their weight in gold.

While these recipes have been tested by the Old-Style community, what suits one person's taste won't always hit the spot with the next, so feel free to vary the measurements and ingredients. And of course anyone with an allergy to particular foods should avoid recipes containing those ingredients. For more recipes go to the Old-Style index thread at www.moneysavingexpert.com/osrecipes

SOUPS

Potato Soup   Serves 6–8

Large knob of butter and a tsp of oil
1 large onion
6–8 fist-sized potatoes
570–850ml (1–½ pints) stock (chicken or vegetable is fine)
Small tub of fresh cream
Handful of parsley, chopped finely

◆   *Melt butter and oil in a large pot (oil prevents butter burning but*
    keeps the taste nice).
◆   *Finely chop the onion and sweat gently in the oil mix.*
◆   *Peel and cut the potatoes into rough pieces and toss in the hot oil*
    mix. Pour on 1 pint of stock and cook until potatoes are tender.
    Whizz in a blender until smooth. You may need to add more stock at
    this stage as the soup tends to thicken.
◆   *Gently heat through again before serving. Serve with a drizzle of*
    cream and some parsley sprinkled on top and Melba toast on the
    side. You can also add leeks to this to make potato and leek soup.

Cream of Mushroom Soup   Serves 6

55g (2oz) butter
1 small onion, chopped finely
255g (9oz) sliced mushrooms
Salt and freshly ground black pepper
30g (1oz) plain flour
450ml (16fl oz) chicken or vegetable stock
To serve: 140ml (5fl oz) milk, 140ml (5fl oz) single cream, 3–4
    mushrooms, sliced and sautéed in butter

◆ *Melt half the butter in a pan. Add the onion and cook gently, stirring until softened.*

◆ *Add the mushrooms with a little salt and pepper and cook until softened. (Cooking the mushrooms until they are slightly caramelised gives a really nice flavour.)*

◆ *Melt the remaining butter in another pan. Stir in the flour and cook, stirring, for 1–2 minutes.*

◆ *Gradually stir in the stock and bring to the boil. Cook, stirring, for 2–3 minutes then add the mushrooms and onions. Purée the soup.*

◆ *To serve, stir in the milk and cream and check the seasoning. Garnish with the sautéed mushrooms.*

Carrot Soup

Serves 4

5–6 carrots, chopped
2 medium-sized potatoes, chopped
1 red onion, chopped finely
1 clove of garlic, crushed
Salt and black pepper
1 stock cube

- *Boil the carrots and potatoes until soft (no need to remove the skins – just wash well).*
- *Cook the onion and garlic in a little butter.*
- *Put everything into a blender with some black pepper and salt.*
- *Add a stock cube to the water that was used to cook the carrots and potatoes (this way you've got some of the goodness back that leached out during cooking). Add a little of the stock to the mixture in the blender.*
- *Blend and then serve. (Can be frozen once cooked.)*

Broccoli and Almond Soup

Serves 6–8

30g (1oz) butter
2 cloves of garlic, crushed
1 onion, diced
225g (8oz) potatoes, diced
75ml (2½ fl oz) white wine

700ml (1¼ pints) vegetable stock
2 heads broccoli
140ml (5fl oz) double cream
70g (2½ oz) flaked almonds, toasted
1 handful parsley, chopped finely
Salt and freshly ground black pepper
To garnish: 1 tbsp parsley (chopped) and 60ml (2fl oz) double cream

◆ *Melt the butter in a large pan. Wait until it's foaming then add the garlic and onion and fry gently for 2–3 minutes (until softened but not browned).*

◆ *Add the potatoes, white wine and stock. Bring to the boil and simmer for 5 minutes.*

◆ *Chop the broccoli into small pieces and add to the pan. Cook for a further 6–8 minutes until the vegetables are soft.*

◆ *Add the cream and half of the almonds, together with the parsley.*

◆ *Remove from the heat and leave to cool slightly. Blend in a food processor until smooth, and then return the soup to the pan and season to taste with salt and freshly ground black pepper.*

◆ *To serve, spoon into bowls and top with the remaining toasted almonds and a little parsley and lightly whipped double cream.*

VEGETARIAN RECIPES

Veggie Cottage Pie　　　　　　　　　　　　Serves 4

1 clove of garlic
1 leek
2 carrots
Cooking oil
1 tbsp flour
285ml ('/₂ pint) vegetable stock
115g (4oz) red lentils
395g (14oz) tin of baked beans
395g (14oz) tin of chopped tomatoes
Salt and black pepper
Potatoes for mash

◆　Preheat the oven to 190°C/375°F/Gas Mark 5.

◆　Crush the garlic; chop the leek and carrots into small cubes.

◆　Heat 1 tbsp of oil in a pan and add the garlic, leek and carrots and
　　sauté for a couple of minutes. Add the flour to the pan and cook for
　　another minute, stirring.

◆　Stir in the veggie stock, bring to the boil and then simmer until the
　　liquid has thickened.

◆　Stir in the red lentils, baked beans and chopped tomatoes. Season to
　　taste. Transfer to a casserole dish and put in the oven for about an hour.

◆　Peel, chop and boil potatoes and mash with milk and butter when
　　cooked. Remove the casserole and spoon mashed potato over the

top, then return to the oven for 10 minutes or until browned. Serve
with crusty bread.

Potato Bake   Serves 6

6–7 medium-sized potatoes, peeled
1 large tin of baked beans in tomato sauce (you could use 2 standard-
       size tins instead)
1 large onion, sliced thinly
2–3 tomatoes, sliced thinly
1 tbsp margarine for dotting over the top
1 tbsp sesame seeds for sprinkling on the top

Other optional layers:
1–2 cups of leftover rice mixed with some soya milk and herbs
Sliced mushrooms mixed with a little vegetable oil and 2 cloves of
       crushed garlic
1 tin of sweetcorn
1 pack spinach

◆   *Parboil the potatoes for 5–6 minutes until starting to soften. Slice
    thinly then place a layer at the base of a large casserole dish. Add a
    layer of beans and onion and repeat till all used up.*

◆   *You can add other layers (using anything lurking at the back of your
    cupboard) like garlic, mushrooms, sweetcorn and spinach but make
    the last layer of potatoes.*

◆ *Spread the tomato slices on top, dot with marg and sprinkle with sesame seeds. Bake for an hour at 190°C/375°F/Gas Mark 5 until the the potatoes are soft.*

Basque Ratatouille   Serves 4

225g (½ lb) onions, peeled and chopped finely
2 cloves of garlic, crushed
2 tbsp olive oil
455g (1lb) courgettes or marrow, washed and sliced
455g (1lb) tomatoes, chopped
1 red pepper, de-seeded and sliced
1 tsp fresh parsley, chopped
Salt and pepper

◆ *Cook the onions and garlic very slowly in the oil for about 10–15 minutes so they become translucent and juicy. Then add all the remaining ingredients and simmer with the lid on for about half an hour. Serve straight away.*
◆ *Serve a big dollop with crusty bread as a main course or side dish. Make loads – it's good cold too and freezes well.*

FAIL-SAFE SLOW COOKER RECIPES

Owning a slow cooker is highly rated in Old-Style – easy to use as you can throw in all your meat and veg in the morning before you leave the house, leave it on all day and when you come home you've got a fabulous stew, casserole or soup. There are far too many recipes to mention here but for more go to the Old-Style index thread at www.moneysavingexpert.com/oscompleteslowcookercollection

Whole Chicken   Serves 4–6

1 (1.3–1.5kg/3–3½lb) whole chicken
1 tsp salt
1 tsp paprika
½ tsp pepper
1 tsp olive oil
1 large onion, sliced
1 medium bulb garlic (about 20 cloves)

◆   *In a small bowl, combine the salt, paprika, pepper and oil. Mix to form a paste. Spread evenly over the chicken.*

◆   *Place the sliced onion in slow cooker. Then place the chicken, breast side up, over the onion.*

◆   *Separate the garlic into cloves – do not peel them. Place the garlic cloves in and around the chicken. Cover and cook on a low setting for at least 7 hours or until the chicken is tender and the juices run clear.*

Easy Spaghetti Sauce

Serves 8–10

225g (8oz) Italian sausage
455g (1lb) lean minced beef
Cooking oil
2 tins (395g/14oz each) of diced tomatoes with juice
1 cup chopped onion
1 tin (225g/8oz) of tomato sauce
1 tin (170g/6oz) of tomato purée
½ cup chopped green pepper
1–2 tbsp sugar
1–2 tsp salt, or to taste
2 cloves of garlic, crushed
2 tsp dried leaf basil
Dash of ground red pepper or red pepper flakes, if desired

◆ *Remove sausage from casings and brown in a heavy frying pan along with the minced beef with a little oil. Break up the sausage and beef while browning; drain well. Add the sausage and beef to the slow cooker, along with all remaining ingredients.*

◆ *Cover and cook on a low setting for 8–10 hours or high for 4–5 hours. This sauce can be frozen if you don't eat it all.*

Moroccan Lamb Stew   Serves 6

680g (1½lb) lamb stewing meat
1 onion, chopped
1 celery stalk, sliced thinly
1 clove of garlic, pressed
395g (14oz) tin of diced tomatoes
80ml (3fl oz) chicken stock
⅓ cup raisins
2 tbsp tomato purée
¼ tsp turmeric
¼ tsp red pepper flakes or chilli powder
¼ tsp pepper

◆   *Combine all the ingredients and cook on high for 4–5 hours or low for
8–10 hours.*

MAIN COURSES

Tuna Pasta Bake   Serves 4

½ an onion, chopped
Cooking oil
395g (14oz) tin of 'value' chopped tomatoes
Pinch of mixed herbs
2 dessertspoons of cream cheese

395g (14oz) tin of tuna, drained
1 small tin of sweetcorn
455g (1lb) freshly cooked pasta shapes
Grated cheese

◆ *Soften the onion in a little oil. Add the tomatoes and pinch of herbs.
Cook down and then liquidise to make a purée.*
◆ *Add the cream cheese, let it melt in then add the tuna. Add the
sweetcorn, warm through and add to cooked pasta. Sprinkle with
cheese and grill.*
◆ *You can also add a crushed bag of plain crisps for a crunchy topping
and a bit of salad or bread on the side.*

Shepherd's Pie   Serves 6

'This is a great one for the kids. They love it with veg and gravy.'

Potatoes for mash
1 onion, sliced
455g (1lb) minced lamb
395g (14oz) tin of chopped tomatoes
395g (14oz) tin of baked beans
Grated Cheddar

◆ *Preheat oven to 200°C/400°F/Gas mark 6.*
◆ *Boil the potatoes for mashing.*

- Fry the onion and mince. When cooked through, add the tomatoes and beans and simmer for 3–5 minutes.
- Transfer to an ovenproof dish, then mash the spuds and add to the top.
- Either bake for 20 minutes with some grated Cheddar on top, or freeze and use later. (If cooking from frozen, get it out the night before to defrost then cook for 30 minutes with Cheddar on top.)

1970s Family Risotto!   Serves 4

'This is a recipe my Mum used throughout my childhood from a 1970s magazine article on "feeding ravenous kids" (that was us!). She used spam, tinned ham or (very often on Monday) leftover chicken, which was GORGEOUS!'

1 tbsp oil
1 small onion, chopped
1 tomato, chopped
55g (2oz) mushrooms, chopped
225g (8oz) long-grain rice
570ml (1 pint) water or stock
170g (6oz) diced cooked ham, chicken, sausages, pork or a mixture of all four
Salt and pepper
To garnish: 1 tbsp chopped parsley

- Heat the oil and fry the onion, tomato and mushrooms for 2–3 minutes.
- Add the remaining ingredients except the parsley.
- Bring to the boil, cover and let it simmer gently, stirring occasionally, for 15–20 minutes, or until the rice has absorbed all the liquid.
- Turn into a serving dish and sprinkle with chopped parsley.

Chinese Chicken   Serves 4

8 chicken thighs, skin on
6 tbsp wine (red or white)
3 tbsp dark soy sauce
1 tbsp water
1 tbsp sugar
1 tsp mustard

- Preheat the oven to 190°C/375°F/Gas Mark 5.
- In a casserole dish, put all the ingredients except the chicken and mix well.
- Add the chicken thighs and coat well with the mixture.
- Put the lid on the casserole dish and cook for an hour. Remove the lid and return the casserole to the oven for about 30 minutes to crisp the skin.
- Serve with veg of choice and mashed potatoes to mop up the gravy.

Spaghetti Carbonara   Serves 2

2 turkey steaks
Cooked spaghetti
1 small onion, sliced
Mushrooms, sliced
Cooking oil
1 egg
Parmesan cheese

◆ *Grill the turkey steaks and cook the spaghetti.*
◆ *Put the onion, mushrooms and spaghetti into a frying pan with a little oil and cook gently.*
◆ *Beat the egg and add to the pan once the onion and mushrooms have softened. Chop the turkey steaks and add to the pan.*
◆ *Once the egg is cooked, serve, sprinkled with Parmesan cheese.*

Basic Bolognaise Sauce   Serves 4–6

'I do this one from memory and you can pretty much add anything else from the cupboard and double up the quantities to freeze it.'

455g (1lb) mince
1 onion, chopped finely
1 clove of garlic, crushed
395g (14oz) tin of tomatoes

1 tbsp tomato purée
1 stock cube
Dried mixed herbs
Mushrooms, sliced

◆ *Brown the mince, onion and garlic together.*
◆ *Add the tinned tomatoes, tomato purée, stock cube, sprinkling of mixed herbs and mushrooms.*
◆ *Put the lid on until cooked thoroughly. If it's too runny keep the lid off for 10 minutes to reduce a bit.*
◆ *Serve with spaghetti.*

Chicken and Aubergine Bake   Serves 4

1 large aubergine, sliced
285g (10oz) potatoes, sliced
4 chicken breasts, skinned and boned
Seasoned flour
Oil for frying
15g (½ oz) butter
2 onions, sliced
1 tsp fresh thyme
Salt and pepper

For the sauce
30g (1oz) butter

2 tbsp flour
140ml (5fl oz) milk
140ml (5fl oz) chicken stock
85g (3oz) cheese
225g (8oz) tomatoes, sliced

◆ *Sprinkle the aubergines with salt. Parboil the potatoes and drain. Beat the chicken between clingfilm to flatten slightly. Dust with flour. Preheat the oven to 180°C/350°F/Gas Mark 4.*

◆ *Heat 3 tbsp oil in a large pan and fry the aubergines in batches for 2–3 minutes, adding more oil if necessary. Drain on kitchen paper. Add 1 tbsp oil and the butter to the pan and fry the chicken until browned. Remove with a slotted spoon, add the onions and fry until soft. Add the thyme and season to taste.*

◆ *For the sauce, melt the butter in a pan, stir in the flour and cook for 1 minute. Stir in the milk, stock and cheese and cook until thickened.*

◆ *Make layers with vegetables, chicken , tomatoes, onions and sauce. Bake in the oven for 1 hour 20 minutes.*

CASSEROLES AND STEWS

Spiced Beef and Beans   Serves 6

'A great recipe which can easily be adapted to cook in a slow cooker for dinner after work.'

455g (1lb) braising steak, chopped into bite-sized pieces
Cooking oil
1 tsp ground coriander
½ tsp ground cumin
¼ tsp ground ginger
1–2 tsp chilli powder according to taste
1 onion
1 red pepper
2 cloves of garlic
1 tin (395g/14oz) of red kidney beans (or other beans if preferred)
285ml (½ pint) beef stock
1 tin (395g/14oz) of chopped tomatoes
2 tbsp tomato purée

◆   *In a pan, brown the meat all over briefly in a little oil. Then add the
    powdered spices, stir and turn the heat down. (You don't need flour
    as the spices thicken it up.)*

◆   *Chop up the onion and pepper, and crush the garlic. Drain and rinse
    the beans, and make up the stock.*

◆   *Add the stock, tomatoes, pepper, onion, tomato purée and garlic to
    the beef. Bring to the boil then pour into a casserole dish. Cook at
    180°C/350°F/Gas Mark 4 for 2–2½ hours.*

Sausage Casserole

Serves 8

'About 50 pence a serving.'

1 pack value sausages
Cooking oil
1 pack sausage casserole mix (Coleman's is good but any will do)
2 medium onions
2 carrots
2 leeks
2 green peppers
2 pints of water
225g ('½ lb) mushrooms

◆ Preheat the oven to about 200°C/400°F/Gas Mark 6.

◆ Brown the sausages in a little oil, chop all the veggies and throw everything into the biggest casserole dish you can find. Cook until you can't wait any longer, making sure everything is totally hot before serving (at least an hour).

◆ Serve with mash or jacket spuds or crusty bread.

◆ For a thicker sauce add tomato purée, another packet of casserole mix or a little cornflour mixed with water. Don't reduce the amount of water or you'll end up with dried-out mushrooms and chewy sausages.

Boeuf Bourguignon   Serves 8

900g (2lb) stewing steak, cut into 5cm (1-inch) squares
3 tbsp olive oil
1 onion, sliced
1 heaped tbsp plain flour
425ml (15fl oz) red Burgundy wine
2 cloves of garlic, chopped
2 sprigs of thyme
1 bay leaf
340g (12oz) small onions
Salt and pepper
225g (8oz) streaky bacon, chopped
115g (4oz) flat mushrooms

- ◆ *Preheat the oven to 140°C/275°F/Gas Mark 1.*
- ◆ *Heat 2 tbsp oil in a flameproof casserole and brown the beef. Remove from the casserole dish and add the sliced onion, cooking gently until it begins to soften.*
- ◆ *Return the meat to the casserole and add the flour, then pour in the wine, add the garlic, herbs and small onions. Season to taste. Place in the preheated oven for 2 hours.*
- ◆ *Fry the bacon and add to the casserole with the mushrooms. Cook for another hour. Serve.*

Creamy Pork Chops Serves 6

6 pork chops
Salt and pepper, to taste
Garlic powder, to taste
2–3 tbsp plain flour
Cooking oil
1 large onion, cut into ¼-inch slices
2 cubes chicken bouillon
500ml (18fl oz) boiling water
2 tbsp plain flour
230ml (8fl oz) soured cream

- ◆ *Season the chops with salt, pepper and garlic powder then dredge in flour. In a frying pan over medium heat, lightly brown the chops in a small amount of oil then place in a slow cooker and top with onion slices. Dissolve the bouillon cubes in boiling water and pour over the chops. Cook on low for 6–7 hours.*

- ◆ *After the chops have cooked, remove from the slow cooker and keep warm. In a bowl blend 2 tbsp flour with the soured cream, and mix into the meat juices. Turn the slow cooker to high for 15–30 minutes until the sauce is slightly thickened. Serve the sauce over the pork chops.*

MEALS FOR ONE AND LIGHT SNACKS

Post-pub Grub

170g (6oz) spaghetti (or any old pasta)
Olive oil (just a splash)
Finely chopped garlic (or garlic powder/granules)
Freshly grated Parmesan (or any old cheese)
Fresh basil leaves, torn (or anything to add flavour such as scrapings
    from the bottom of the pesto jar, sun-dried tomatoes, capers,
    anchovies, fresh tomatoes chopped small, dried herbs)

◆ *Cook the pasta as directed (about 12 minutes is a good guess). Drain
    and add olive oil along with the rest of the ingredients.*

◆ *Give the pan a good shake and reheat everything gently. Eat straight
    from the pan (saves washing up!), preferably with a fork.*

Camembert Easy Lunch

1 small, good-quality, boxed Camembert cheese
A few drops of wine
1 clove of garlic (optional)
Some really fresh bread

◆ *Remove the cheese from its wrapping, prick the top a few times with
    a knife and add a few drops of wine so that it soaks in. You can also*

rub garlic on it if you like. Put the lid back on the box and bake in a medium oven for 25 minutes.

◆ *Put the cheese in the middle of the table and eat by dipping the bread into the melted cheese. Great with pickles, salad and olives.*

Vegetarian Cheese 'n' Onion Sandwich Filling

Chop up a tiny bit of onion, mix with a couple of ounces of grated cheese and a couple of dessertspoons of mayonnaise and a shake of celery salt (if you've got it). Keeps in the fridge for a couple of days and great on burgers and jacket spuds as well as sandwiches.

Easy Walnut Sauce for Pasta

'This is a great one for the hot weather as there's no cooking involved. You also get to use up your stale-ish bread!'

3 slices of bread, crusts and all
2 small handfuls walnuts
1 clove of garlic
5–6 basil leaves
3 sprigs parsley
Big glug of olive oil, about 3 tbsp
Big glug of milk, as above
To serve: pasta, peas, runner beans, tomatoes, grated cheese

◆ *Blitz that little lot together in a food processor. This can then be thinned to your desired consistency with a little extra milk, or with some reserved pasta cooking water.*

◆ *Toss the sauce with hot pasta and add peas, runner beans, tomatoes if you like and serve with grated cheese. Extra parsley is a good idea to tame the garlic.*

Corned Beef Hash

'An ideal meal for one. You can jazz it up if you've got onions or peas. Basic but yummy, it costs a grand total of £1.41.'

1 small tin of corned beef
1 carrot, cubed
1 potato, cubed
1 Oxo cube dissolved in 140ml (¼ pint) of liquid

◆ *Heat 2 tablespoons of oil in a frying pan and, when it's smoking hot, add the potato until browned.*

◆ *Add some seasoning, the carrot and the corned beef, followed by the Oxo cube stock.*

◆ *Simmer until the liquid has disappeared and the ingredients are fully heated and serve.*

Mushroom Risotto

1 small pack (approx. 20g/¾oz) dried porcini mushrooms
2 tbsp olive oil
Knob of butter
1 medium onion, chopped finely
1 stick of celery, chopped finely
4–6 brown cap or chestnut mushrooms, cleaned and sliced
160g (5½oz) risotto rice
Couple of glugs of sherry/Madeira or red wine
Approx. 340ml (12fl oz) hot vegetable stock
85g (3oz) Parmesan cheese (fresh pukka stuff), grated
To garnish: a few basil leaves and Parmesan shavings

◆ Put the dried mushrooms in a bowl and cover with warm water. Leave to stand for about half an hour. Remove mushrooms and chop quite finely. Strain and reserve the soaking liquid.

◆ Heat the oil and butter in a pan. Add the onion and celery and cook for 5 minutes.

◆ Add the brown cap or chestnut mushrooms and the porcini mushrooms and cook for another 5 minutes.

◆ Stir in the rice. Cook gently for a few more minutes until the individual rice grains are coated with the oil. Now prepare to stand by your cooker for the next 20 minutes or so!

◆ Add the soaking liquid and the sherry/Madeira or red wine and stir. Bring to the boil and simmer gently. As the liquid is absorbed, add a little of the stock. Keep stirring, adding more stock when necessary.

The stock needs to be kept hot, say in another pan on the cooker. Proceed in this way, adding a little stock at a time, until the rice is tender (about 20 minutes).

◆ *Add grated Parmesan and keep stirring for another 2–3 minutes. The finished result should be gloopy and runny as the Italians do it and not stiff.*

◆ *Serve with shavings of Parmesan on top along with a few torn basil leaves.*

Leeks and Bacon

3 leeks
6 rashers of bacon
2 hardboiled eggs
Cheese sauce
Grated cheese

◆ *Cut the leeks into three and boil till soft.*
◆ *Grill the bacon and wrap around the leeks.*
◆ *Halve the eggs and put on top of the leeks and bacon.*
◆ *Pour the cheese sauce over and top with grated cheese.*
◆ *Cook for 30 minutes in a moderate oven (around 180°C/350°f/Gas mark 4) till browned.*

Pizza Toast

'A filling snack, quick lunch or great supper. Makes enough for one person.'

½ an onion
Olive oil
Salt and pepper
Chopped herbs or dried oregano
Few slices of mushroom, pepper or whatever, if liked
115ml (4fl oz) cup of tomato sauce (leftover from spag bol or out of a jar)
2 slices of bread
Handful of grated cheese or pieces of mozzarella

◆   *Chop the onion and cook in a little olive oil in a small pan. Season to taste, then add the herbs and any other veg.*
◆   *When softened, add the sauce and simmer for a few minutes.*
◆   *Toast the bread on one side.*
◆   *Spread the tomato mixture over the un-toasted side of the bread. Top with cheese and grill.*

Pasta, Beans and Cheese

*'Carbs, fibre and protein on a plate! Under £1 a portion, around
10 minutes to make and great for a quick snack or student grub.'*

Pasta shapes (fresh or dried)
1 tin of baked beans
Grated cheese (can be value or leftover cheese)

◆   *Boil up some pasta, heat the beans, pour over the cooked pasta and
    grate some cheese on top.*

GREAT 'LEFTOVER' RECIPES

Chicken Louisiana   Serves 4

170g (6oz) long-grain rice
450ml (16fl oz) chicken stock
1 tbsp oil
3 rashers of bacon, chopped
1 large onion, sliced
1 green or red pepper, sliced
395g (14oz) tin of chopped tomatoes
Approx. 340g (12oz) leftover chicken
2 cooked spicy sausages, sliced
Seasoning

- Put the rice and stock in a pan and bring to the boil. Cover and simmer gently until the rice is tender and the liquid has been absorbed.
- Meanwhile, heat the oil in another pan and fry the bacon, onion and pepper. Stir in the tomatoes, chicken and sausages, season to taste, add the rice, stir and cook for 10 minutes; then serve.

Bacon Pie   Serves 4–6

'For a variation, add whatever vegetables you like and vary the condensed soup flavours – tomato makes a nice sauce. You can also top with cheese just before serving.'

1 packet (Lidl) bacon misshapes
1 large onion
1 clove of garlic, finely chopped
Cooking oil
1 cup of frozen peas
285ml (10fl oz) pot of single cream
1 tin of condensed soup (mushroom is ideal)
Leftover mash

- Chop the bacon into pieces and cook until just done.
- Finely chop the onion and soften in a little oil, together with the garlic. Add the frozen peas and cook until just tender.

- ◆ Mix the cream and soup together. (You can thin the soup with mostly anything – cream, milk or even water).
- ◆ Place the bacon, peas and onion mix in the bottom of a casserole dish. Pour the soup mix over and allow to cool.
- ◆ Fluff up the leftover mash with a fork and spread over the bacon mix when cool.
- ◆ Cook at 200°C/400°F/Gas Mark 6 for approximately 30–40 minutes until bubbling hot and the potato is browned and crispy.

Cheddar Cheese and Vegetable Bake   Serves 2

3 tbsp oil
1 medium onion, chopped finely
1 small red pepper, chopped finely
1 small orange pepper, chopped finely
3 sticks celery, sliced
340g (12oz) mushrooms, sliced
225g (8oz) whole-wheat breadcrumbs
170g (6oz) mature Cheddar, grated
1 large egg
Salt and pepper

- ◆ Preheat the oven to 190°C/375°F/Gas Mark 5. Lightly grease a 1.2-litre (2-pint) ovenproof dish.
- ◆ Heat the oil gently and fry the onion, peppers and celery for 5 minutes. Add the mushrooms and fry for another 1–2 minutes.

- ◆ *Remove the pan from the heat and stir in 170g (6oz) breadcrumbs and 115g (4oz) cheese. Beat the egg with salt and pepper and add to the pan, stirring. Mix everything together well.*
- ◆ *Spoon the mixture into the greased baking dish and level with the back of a spoon.*
- ◆ *Mix together the remaining cheese and breadcrumbs and sprinkle over the top. Bake for 25 minutes. Can be eaten hot or cold.*

PUDDINGS AND DESSERTS

Rhubarb and Strawberry Crumble   Serves 4–6

455g (1lb) rhubarb (fresh from the garden), cut in 2.5cm (1-inch)
    pieces
A few strawberries (about 6–8)
70–100g (2½–3½oz) granulated sugar
170g (6oz) plain flour
70g (2½oz) butter
55g (2oz) caster sugar

- ◆ *Preheat the oven to 190°C/375°F/Gas Mark 5.*
- ◆ *Put the fruit into a 1.2-litre (2-pint) oven-proof dish in layers with the granulated sugar.*
- ◆ *Sift the flour into a bowl. Rub the butter into the flour until the mixture resembles fine breadcrumbs. Stir in the caster sugar.*
- ◆ *Sprinkle the crumble mixture thickly and evenly over the fruit. Press*

> *down lightly with the palm of your hand then smooth the top with a knife.*

◆ *Bake for 15 minutes. Reduce the temperature to 180°C/350°F/Gas Mark 4 for a further 45 minutes or until the top is lightly browned.*

Bread and Butter Pudding   Serves 4–6

1 medium brioche loaf (20p yellow-stickered in Morrisons)
Handful of currants
1 apple, chopped pretty small
Squirty honey
Butter
340–570ml (¾–1 pint) milk
2 eggs
2 tbsp granulated sugar
Small splash vanilla essence
Demerara sugar

◆ *Butter the bread, then stack in a greased Pyrex dish in layers, scattering some currants, apple and a thin swirl of honey between each layer.*

◆ *Stick a decent-sized knob of butter in a saucepan. Add the milk, eggs, sugar and vanilla essence and keep mixing until hot and thickened. Then pour straight over the bread.*

◆ *Shake the dish about, and maybe poke some holes in the mixture and lift with a knife to make sure the custard gets to the bottom. Then sprinkle with a bit of Demerara and put in a medium oven*

*(around 170°C/325°F/Gas Mark 3) until nice and brown. Enjoy with
ice cream!*

Fifteens   Makes 12-16

*'So easy to make you can let your kids do it at the weekend to keep them
amused!'*

15 digestive biscuits
15 glacé cherries, chopped
15 marshmallows, chopped
1 tin of condensed milk
Desiccated coconut

◆   *Crush the digestive biscuits and add the cherries and marshmallows.
    Stir in the condensed milk until the mixture will hardly move!*

◆   *Sprinkle some coconut on a piece of greaseproof paper. Spoon some
    of the biscuit mixture on top of the coconut, then sprinkle more
    coconut on top. Roll up like a sausage inside the greaseproof paper
    and seal the ends (I roll tinfoil round mine.) Place in the fridge for
    2–3 hours until firm. Unwrap and cut into slices.*

Chewy Fruit Muesli Slice

Makes 8 wedges

½ cup dried apricots, chopped
1 eating apple, cored and grated
¼ cup Swiss-style muesli
160ml (6fl oz) cup apple juice
1 tbsp soft margarine

◆ Preheat the oven to 190°C/375°F/Gas Mark 5.
◆ Place all the ingredients in a large bowl and mix well.
◆ Press the mixture into a 20-cm (8-inch) non-stick cake tin and bake for 35–40 minutes until lightly browned and firm.
◆ Mark the muesli slice into 8 wedges and allow to cool in the pan.

Nutty Meringues

Makes 6–8

1 egg white
½ cup caster sugar
½ cup rice crispies
1 cup cornflakes

◆ Whisk the egg white until stiff. Add the sugar and whisk till stiff again, then fold in the rice crispies and cornflakes.
◆ Place dessertspoonfuls of the mixture on a baking sheet lined with parchment/greaseproof paper. Bake in a slow oven (150°C/300°F/Gas Mark 2) for 25–30 minutes. When cold, sandwich together with butter icing.

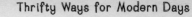

Fruit Fluff   Serves 6

'I wanted a quick pudding that was cold for a warm summer's day.
Suddenly I remembered a recipe I used years ago when the kids were small.'

200g (7oz) a tin of evaporated milk
1 jelly tablet

◆   Put the evaporated milk in the fridge to cool. Then empty it into a
    large bowl and whisk with a hand-held mixer until it has fluffed up to
    twice the volume.

◆   Melt a jelly tablet in a tiny bit of water in the microwave on high for
    1 minute then, with the whisk going at full speed, whisk the melted
    jelly into the evaporated milk. It will bulk up quite a bit more so
    make sure you have a BIG bowl.

◆   When all the jelly has been mixed in, pour into small dishes or a large
    dish and chill in the fridge. Serve with a blob of ice cream or, if you
    feel really sinful, pour double cream over the top, or whip some
    cream and pipe rosettes around the edge. I have done it with orange
    jelly in a big bowl and decorated the top with mandarin oranges and
    whipped cream; you can do the same with fresh strawberries if you
    have just a few left.

Banana Bread   Makes 1–2 loaves

*'Great for using up those over-ripe bananas. Freezes well and is lovely
sliced, toasted and dripping with melted butter.'*

3 very ripe bananas (almost walking)
Pinch of salt
170g (6oz) melted butter
1 tsp bicarbonate of soda dissolved in 1 tbsp water
170g (6oz) caster sugar
1 egg
255–285g (9–10oz) plain flour

◆   *Smash the bananas (a food processor is great for this recipe).*
◆   *Add the remaining ingredients and mix together. Pour into 2 greased
    or paper-lined 1lb loaf tins or 1 2lb tin.*
◆   *Bake in a moderate oven (180°C/350°F/Gas Mark 4) for 45 minutes.*

Proper Custard   Makes 285ml (½ pint)

285ml (½ pint) milk
1 vanilla pod
4 egg yolks
30g (1oz) sugar

◆   *Save 3 tbsp of the milk. Place the remaining milk and vanilla pod in* a saucepan, bring almost to the boil, remove from the heat and rest for 15 minutes.

◆ Put the egg yolks, sugar and saved milk in a bowl and beat until thick and creamy.

◆ Remove the vanilla pod from the rested sauce and pour onto the egg mixture.

◆ Strain back into the saucepan and cook, stirring, until it coats the back of a spoon.

◆ Serve hot or cold. Will be much thicker if left to cool.

PACKED LUNCHES

◆ Spuds and a container of cheese and coleslaw or beans for nutritious, cheap and easy lunch.

◆ Stock up on ready-meals when they're reduced in the supermarket and freeze till you need them – great if you've got a microwave at work.

◆ Brilliant for using up 'leftovers' from the night before. If you never end up with any left, make a bit more so you've got enough for an extra portion.

◆ Packs of 'value' Chinese noodles take up next to no space, and are ready in minutes and filling.

◆ Add a pack of 'value' noodles to a tin of soup to make it into a meal.

◆ Make up a load of stew, spaghetti bolognaise or whatever and portion out into small containers for the freezer.

Cheap and Cheerful Sandwich Fillings
(as voted by Old-Stylers)

If you just can't do without your home-made sarnie and aren't
counting the calories, here are some Old-Style fillings . . .

- *Marmite and cheese*
- *Peanut butter and chocolate spread*
- *Crisps – any flavour!*
- *Chicken paste and ready-salted crisps*
- *Condensed milk sandwiches (apparently it's very thick so easy to eat!)*
- *Thick white bread, butter and sugar (rots your teeth but tastes good so we're told!)*

HANDY KITCHEN EQUIPMENT

What's your 'can't manage without it' kitchen gadget? We've all got
gadgets and gizmos hidden away that rarely, if ever, see the light of day.
Maybe it's that 'hard to clean' sandwich toaster or the food processor
stuck at the back of the cupboard?

You've got to find what works for you, but here's the equipment
most highly rated by Old-Stylers.

Food Processor

Great for mixing anything from smoothies, soups and pastry to chopping onions and grinding coffee and fresh whole spices. It doesn't have to be an all-singing all-dancing version – even the humble £4.99 Tesco value blender is highly rated, and at that price it won't need to last a lifetime.

Slow Cooker

Handy for those meals where you can bung it all in first thing in the morning and then come back at 6pm to a gorgeous-smelling casserole. It can be used for joints, stews, casseroles, curries, meatloaf, soups, chilli and rice pudding. The main advice here is always to buy bigger than you think you'll need – families will grow and you can always make more to use up the next day or freeze.

Bread-maker

Depending on which model you've got, they can be multi-purpose – some can be used to make fruitcake, pizza dough, rolls and even jam! Although they're highly rated, it can be a case of 'you get what you pay for' here – some of the cheaper ones have been known to produce bread resembling house bricks.

George Foreman-style Grill

These are good for toasties, kids' sausages, chicken, bacon and hash browns, but not so good with very thick sausages or chops. They can also be a pain to clean if you don't do it while still hot.

STORE CUPBOARD ESSENTIALS

If you've got the basic store cupboard essentials you'll be able to whiz up most meals in minutes, so what should you be stocking up on? Most of the meals in this chapter rely heavily on many of the items in the store cupboard basics listed below.

In the Fridge

Butter, cheese, eggs and milk – you can make anything from omelettes to sauces.

In the Store Cupboard

◆   *Rice, pasta, potatoes – the staple of many Old-Style meals*
◆   *Olive oil – for salad dressings and cooking*
◆   *Flour – makes a cheap sauce thickener rather than buying those 'thickening granules'*

- ◆ *Tinned chopped tomatoes for pasta sauces, soups and curries – value tins are under 20p each*
- ◆ *Oxo cubes for sauces, gravy and beefing up watery dishes*
- ◆ *Cook-in sauces, like Dolmio – a good standby but choose cheaper, supermarket own-brand ones – or make your own*
- ◆ *Campbell's condensed soup – good for casserole sauces so keep an eye out for BOGOF offers (the Mediterranean one is good for pizza topping)*
- ◆ *Tinned tuna – great for making pasta bakes or sandwiches, jacket potato toppings...*
- ◆ *Skimmed milk powder – for making emergency sauces when you've run out of milk*

Stash Cupboard

If it's there for the taking... here's how to be thrifty when you're out. From McDonalds' cutlery to raiding the bathroom if you're lucky enough to stay in a posh hotel for the night – here's what to take for your stash cupboard.

- ◆ *Creamer pots from coffee bars*
- ◆ *Salt, mayonnaise and sauce sachets and serviettes from burger bars – handy for picnics*
- ◆ *Tea, coffee and hot chocolate sachets and biscuits from hotels*
- ◆ *Individual jams you get in hotels – great for picnics or gift hampers*
- ◆ *Wet wipes from KFC*

◆ *Herbal fruit teas from hotels*

◆ *Sachets of tartar sauce or any sauces you don't buy because only one of you likes it – burger bars and pubs are great for picking these up*

◆ *Sachets of sugar – worth picking up if you're a non-sugar household for when visitors come round*

◆ *Spare sandwiches from office client lunches – wrap them up and take them home or enjoy a free lunch*

◆ *Plastic cutlery and straws from McDonalds, M&S and even from flights – great for picnics*

INDEX

THE MONEY DIET
By Martin Lewis, Money Saving Expert

Do you want to cut your bills without cutting back?
Are you fed up with being ripped off?
Do you want more money in your pocket?

The average person spends more money on their telephone bills than stocks and shares – so why do finance books always talk about the markets?

This new, fully revised and updated edition of the original bestseller guarantees you will save tens, hundreds or even thousands of pounds on everything from credit cards and mortgages to mobile phones and DVDs – all without changing your lifestyle.

With crash-diet tips for speedy savings, a healthy eating guide to debt management, case studies and a complete financial fitness for life programme to strengthen your MoneySaving muscles, Martin Lewis can save you £6,000 a year with his fully-researched, easy-to-implement, cutting-edge advice.

☐ The Money Diet   9780091906887   £7.99

FREE POSTAGE AND PACKING
Overseas customers allow £2.00 per paperback

ORDER:

By phone: 01624 677237

By post: Random House Books
c/o Bookpost
PO Box 29
Douglas
Isle of Man IM99 1BQ

By fax: 01624 670923

By email: bookshop@enterprise.net

Cheques (payable to Bookpost) and credit cards accepted

Prices and availability subject to change without notice.
Allow 28 days for delivery.
When placing your order, please mention if you do not wish to
receive any additional information.

www.randomhouse.co.uk